"Like you and your daughter, Queen Esther was once a teen filled with longing, hope, insecurities, and fears. Her secrets of womanhood provide the opportunity to gently lead your girl through the tenuous process of becoming a woman with practicality, pampering, and panache. Many thanks to author Ginger Garrett for this enjoyable tool that's sure to leave a lasting impression on your family. As Garrett says, "Never underestimate the lasting influence of a mom.""

JENN DOUCETTE, author of *The Velveteen Mommy:*
Laughter and Tears from the Toy Box Years

"Ginger Garrett has written a sensitive, interactive guide for moms to raise godly and healthy daughters. Filled with practical ways to connect with and speak into a daughter's life, this is a needed resource to help daughters successfully navigate growing up in today's changing culture."

LINDA MINTLE, PhD

Queen Esther's

SECRETS OF WOMANHOOD

A Biblical Rite of Passage for Your Daughter

GINGER GARRETT

NAVPRESS®

BRINGING TRUTH TO LIFE

OUR GUARANTEE TO YOU

We believe so strongly in the message of our books that we are making this quality guarantee to you. If for any reason you are disappointed with the content of this book, return the title page to us with your name and address and we will refund to you the list price of the book. To help us serve you better, please briefly describe why you were disappointed. Mail your refund request to: NavPress, P.O. Box 35002, Colorado Springs, CO 80935.

The Navigators is an international Christian organization. Our mission is to advance the gospel of Jesus and His kingdom into the nations through spiritual generations of laborers living and discipling among the lost. We see a vital movement of the gospel, fueled by prevailing prayer, flowing freely through relational networks and out into the nations where workers for the kingdom are next door to everywhere.

NavPress is the publishing ministry of The Navigators. The mission of NavPress is to reach, disciple, and equip people to know Christ and make Him known by publishing life-related materials that are biblically rooted and culturally relevant. Our vision is to stimulate spiritual transformation through every product we publish.

ISBN 1-57683-986-9

Cover design by Disciple Design
Cover image by Getty
Creative Team: Terry Behimer, Andrea Christian, Darla Hightower, Arvid Wallen, Kathy Guist

Some of the anecdotal illustrations in this book are true to life and are included with the permission of the persons involved. All other illustrations are composites of real situations, and any resemblance to people living or dead is coincidental.

In the sections of this book about body image and health, this publication is designed to provide accurate information on the subject matter. It is sold with the understanding that the publisher is not engaged in rendering professional services. If professional advice or other expert assistance is required, the services of a competent professional person should be sought.

Unless otherwise identified, all Scripture quotations in this publication are taken from *THE MESSAGE* (MSG). Copyright © 1993, 1994, 1995, 1996, 2000, 2001, 2002. Used by permission of NavPress Publishing Group; Other versions used include: the HOLY BIBLE: NEW INTERNATIONAL VERSION® (NIV®), Copyright © 1973, 1978, 1984 by International Bible Society, used by permission of Zondervan Publishing House, all rights reserved; and the *New American Standard Bible* (NASB), © The Lockman Foundation 1960, 1962, 1963, 1968, 1971, 1972, 1973, 1975, 1977, 1995.

Published in association with the literary agency of Alive Communications, Inc., 7680 Goddard Street, Suite 200, Colorado Springs, CO 80920 (www.alivecommunications.com).

Library of Congress Cataloging-in-Publication Data
Garrett, Ginger, 1968-
  Queen Esther's secrets of womanhood : a biblical rite of passage for
your daughter / Ginger Garrett.
    p. cm.
  Includes bibliographical references.
  ISBN 1-57683-986-9
  1. Bible. O.T. Esther--Criticism, interpretation, etc. 2. Esther,
Queen of Persia. I. Title.
  BS1375.52.G37 2006
  248.8'431--dc22
                               2006016329

Printed in the United States of America

1 2 3 4 5 6 / 10 09 08 07 06

FOR A FREE CATALOG OF NAVPRESS BOOKS & BIBLE STUDIES,
CALL 1-800-366-7788 (USA) OR 1-800-839-4769 (CANADA)

Dedication

To my mom, Carole, and my grandmothers, Eloise and Helen, who taught me everything I should know about being a woman, and to my great-grandmother Mimi—who taught me a little more.

Contents

Introduction

Can you name one thing you learned from listening to bedtime stories as a child?

I can name at least two:

- Even princesses have bad days.
- The prince always shows up, but he misses all the action.

We suffered through the heroine's rejections, applauded her faithful friends, booed the bad guys, and cheered when the prince finally showed up. (Why was he always so late? Was he afraid to ask for directions?) There was no better way to end the day than hearing a book snap closed with the words "Happily Ever After" lingering in the air. How many sweet evenings did we spend as children listening to stories and falling asleep to the sound of our mother's voice? I hope for you it was many such blessed times. The stories we hear as children stay with us all of our lives.

When you became a mom, the tradition of storytelling was automatically passed to you. There was no official proclamation. No one from the government contacted you with papers to sign. It was simply understood: Moms tell stories. Some of us began when our children were still in our wombs, and others of us bought a collection of children's books right after we bought *What to Expect When You're Expecting* or a book from Dr. Spock. Did you anticipate those sweet evenings of stories and relish the idea of introducing them to your daughter? How many wonderful times did you share revisiting the same stories you heard as a child?

Stories and storytelling belong to moms first and forever. It's a wonderful way to share the secrets of life with our daughters. But stories shouldn't end when we run out of fairy tales. That's when the real stories should begin, with real-life heroines, discouragement and triumph, menacing villains, and life truths that are far more transforming than a magic wand.

We all love stories, and we learn by them. If you listen closely at women's dinner parties, lunch dates, or anywhere conversation is happening between us, you'll see an interesting phenomenon at work: One story sparks another. If you tell your friends about a car breakdown on the interstate, someone will respond with a similar harrowing tale. If you share your worst date, someone will respond with her own dating disaster. And secretly, quietly, every woman listening is making mental notes: what to remember, what not to do, and how to learn from the story and move on, incorporating its wisdom and warnings into her life. And in fact, sharing stories may not just reflect the world we've experienced: Storytelling may actually help create it. We become participants in the drama and are instructed and changed as we listen. We respond differently to life and recognize the wise paths not yet taken.

Walter Benjamin, a German theologian, said, "The art of storytelling is reaching its end because the epic side of truth—wisdom—is dying out." When you look around, it does seem as if wisdom is a dying spirit, doesn't it? Our girls are coming of age in a culture that values many things about them over wisdom. But the Bible reminds us that "Wisdom is supreme; therefore get wisdom. Though it cost all you have, get understanding" (Proverbs 4:7, NIV). Wisdom and stories go hand in hand. After all, Jesus relied on stories to impart His wisdom. God Himself is the beloved Storyteller, and many refer to the Bible as a collection of stories—an epic tale of love won, lost, and recovered.

That's why *Queen Esther's Secrets* is centered around a story from the book of Esther found in the Old Testament. We'll let Esther tell us her tale, and this, in turn, will spark your own stories. And your stories will impact your daughter, staying with her long after other words are forgotten.

But of all the books of the Bible, why use the book of Esther? I've been immersed in Esther's story for several years now, researching, dreaming, and piecing facts and history together, trying to listen very closely to what she has to say. And I've concluded that Esther's story is one of the richest in the Bible, and in all of recorded literature, for women. We are introduced to Esther as a young girl and follow her journey from an orphan living in exile to a girl given exactly one year to become beautiful and win a king. She becomes the most powerful woman in the empire and is forced to confront the darkest of evils. Esther's story touches on almost every aspect of life as a woman.

While we're studying Esther's powerful story and preparing you to share your own, we're going to have a great time. This year may become one of the most memorable years in your daughter's life—one that you both reflect on throughout the decades ahead with gratitude and a lot of laughter. After all, stories aren't told best in a dry, sterile environment. Stories between us girls are best shared over coffee and dessert, in the beauty salon, and at the manicurist's table. That's one reason you and your daughter will be talking about *Queen Esther's Secrets* in both spas and coffee shops.

Your daughter has entered into a time of life when what she looks like is more important in the world's eyes than who she is and the inner life of her spirit. She's experiencing the same challenge Esther did. Esther was valued first, and sometimes only, for her appearance. And yet she rose above this preoccupation to become one of the most powerful and beloved heroines of all time. We don't know what she looked like, but we know that she was a woman of faith and courage. In *Queen Esther's Secrets* we'll acknowledge the role beauty plays in our lives, but we'll focus on the eternal impact of character and spirit.

Like Esther's story, where we begin is only a hint of the adventures to come.

Esther's story begins when she is declared beautiful and therefore fit for the king's harem. But her beauty doesn't cause her to live "happily ever after"; it leads her deeper into intrigue and conflict. The world whispers to our girls that the stories of their lives aren't worthwhile unless they are judged as beautiful. Only then can they know acceptance, fulfillment, and security. Only then will they live "happily ever after." If the world were telling the story of Esther, it would begin and end with her being declared beautiful and fit for a king. But because God is telling this story, we see that beauty is only the beginning of Esther's story. She swims against the current toward a new goal.

In the same way, we want our daughters to have the faith to leap forward and push against the unyielding standards that try to define them. Together we'll define beauty as something more than appearance. How we care for and present ourselves is an indicator of what we believe. We'll enjoy pampering ourselves on the outside, but our primary focus is on the transformative and sometimes difficult work of developing true character. Our true beauty is found in who we are in Christ. This is the heart of the story we want our daughters to understand.

Queen Esther's Secrets will meet a basic, urgent need in your daughter's life: helping her feel good in her own skin right now, even while you prepare her for her life ahead as a godly woman. The stories you'll be sharing with her include: what true love is and why it's different from romance, how to understand and handle the changing hormones and moods women experience, how to be confident in the face of fear, and secrets on feeling beautiful even when the world tells her that she's imperfect.

What would you have given as a young teen to have had these secrets and stories passed along to you? How would it have changed you? So often, we didn't get everything we needed, not because it was deliberately withheld, but because it wasn't packaged in a way that got our attention. Perhaps we tuned out vital information because we thought it was just another lecture. Perhaps the stories that could have impacted us fell through the cracks of a crowded life. *Queen Esther's Secrets* gives you a meaningful, fun format that addresses your daughter's core needs. You'll be creating a bond of intimacy just as she enters the most turbulent time of her life.

If you feel a little uneasy about storytelling without a script, that's okay. We'll work through what to share every month and give you lots of hints about how to weave your stories into a memorable evening with your daughter. Stories don't need special effects. They don't even have to be dramatic. They just have to be yours—part of your life experience. Stories are the fabric of the legacy you'll leave your daughter, and that fabric will be as unique as you are. Don't get caught up on remembering exact names, dates, places, or minor details. As my buddy Chip once reminded me, "You're not a social historian." Tell your own story, at your own pace.

Ready?

The first step is already completed. You've bought this book, and your desire has been stirred to pass along wisdom to your daughter in a memorable, life-changing year. Next, you'll need to prepare your daughter. You may want to say something like this:

> *Sweetheart, there are a lot of things I wish I had known at your age. As I got older, I realized that many women in our family, and even in the Bible, had experienced the same things I did, but somehow, these stories never got passed to me. There were stories I didn't hear until it was too late. Life just gets so busy, and as you enter into your teen years and prepare to become a woman, there isn't always time, or the right time, to share the heritage of women with you.*

So every month for one year, I'll give you one day. I'll give you a beauty or spa treatment, or maybe take you shopping for clothes or jewelry. I'll do something that makes you feel good, and beautiful. We'll work together to help bring out God's gift of beauty that is so unique and inspiring in you. And then, we'll go to dinner, or coffee and dessert, and I'll share my stories with you. That's what Queen Esther's Secrets is: one day a month for one year to do something just for you and prepare you for the mysteries and privileges of being a woman. I want to prepare you by passing along all my secret wisdom, all the wisdom of the women in our family, and what we've learned from the women in the Bible. We'll focus on one woman in particular: Esther. Esther was a young girl, about twelve years old or so when her story begins, and you won't believe what happens next. Are you ready for your Esther Year? Let's pick a date to begin, and we'll get ready to start one of the most memorable years of your life: your Esther Year.

How to Lead Your Daughter Through Queen Esther's Secrets

What's the best age to begin Queen Esther's Secrets with my daughter?

This book is geared for moms who have daughters about to enter high school, but the format and questions are so flexible that they can be tailored to any age. I selected the age range of eleven to thirteen for two reasons: (1) It's probably close to Esther's actual age when her story began. (2) It's the age when girls are at a critical turning point in their development. Moms worry about sex, drugs, and alcohol—and the older your daughter gets, the more likely she is to have been exposed to or experimented with these dangers. As your daughter matures, the more her body will change, her friendships will change, and her desires will change. Giving her an initiation into the secrets of womanhood *now* gives you an opportunity to set the foundation she'll need in the years ahead.

If your daughter is older or younger, I've made it easy to shape the program to fit her needs. First, you can tailor the beauty treats to her age by referring to the Resource Guide in the back of the book. For example, an older teen might have fun going with her mom to a spa for a massage together, but a younger teen might be better suited for a skin-care lesson. Next, as you prepare your responses to the discussion questions, you can share what is most appropriate for your girl. Remember, *Queen Esther's Secrets* isn't meant to be highly structured. You decide what to share and what to do—the format allows you to customize the evening and the discussion to make a lasting, loving memory with your daughter.

What are my responsibilities every month during Queen Esther's Secrets?

As the mother of two girls, I know sometimes there's just too much estrogen and not enough time! I've kept the format for *Queen Esther's Secrets* quite simple. There won't be intensive study required, but you will want some private time to collect your thoughts and pray about your time with your daughter. Try to schedule a morning at a coffee shop or in a quiet corner the week before so you have time to reflect and prepare.

You'll begin by reading a short chapter in this book and completing the "Story Stirrers," questions that are meant to help you remember and sort through the life stories you want to share with your daughter. There will also be an opportunity to "Go Back for Seconds" through suggestions for activities that will help you and your daughter further apply that month's lesson. Then you'll arrange for a beauty treat and a place to grab a quiet dinner or dessert. Don't feel any pressure to spend beyond your budget. Many of these beauty treats can be done at home, and finding a quiet place for a coffee and dessert may be more fun, and less expensive, than a full dinner each time. Finally, we'll provide special appointment cards for you to use to invite your daughter to the evening. (These can be found online at www.gingergarrett.com.) You'll fill out the card and give it to your daughter, and the preparations for the evening will be completed.

The emphasis is on creating memorable times together, and I want you to enjoy it in every way. After all, the journey inside *Queen Esther's Secrets* is for moms, too. The time you spend preparing for your evenings with your daughter will be a meaningful time between you and God as you walk through your past and look ahead to your future. You're giving your daughter a great gift, but I hope you take the time to fully receive the gifts of this year as well.

What if I don't feel ready to lead my daughter? What if I still struggle with issues from my own past?

I understand, moms! I struggle with mistakes from my past, too. I don't feel adequate to raise my daughters perfectly. I wonder how God can use me, warts and all. Sometimes I spend more time regretting my decisions than I do figuring out how to share my hard-won wisdom with my daughters. This goes to the heart of what we believe about our salvation: God has rescued us and set us free, but some of us still live as if we're guilty. God has given us the family gems: wisdom, mercy, forgiveness, and hope, but we're not really sure they belong to us. We know intellectually that we've been forgiven, but we live as though we're expecting punishment. In John 8:7-11, Jesus talked about forgiveness to a crowd bent on stoning a guilty woman:

> *They kept at him, badgering him. He straightened up and said, "The sinless one among you, go first: Throw the stone." . . .*
>
> *Hearing that, they walked away, one after another, beginning with the oldest. The woman was left alone. Jesus stood up and spoke to her. "Woman, where are they? Does no one condemn you?"*
>
> *"No one, Master."*
>
> *"Neither do I," said Jesus. "Go on your way. From now on, don't sin."*

Today, there aren't many stone-throwing crowds wandering our streets, but Satan doesn't need them—we've done a marvelous job of throwing stones at ourselves. Jesus has forgiven us, and we need to accept His forgiveness. We don't have to keep a stone on hand for the next time we mess up. Jesus sent the crowd away—let's not invite them to follow us around.

As we raise our daughters, we see our own childhood and adolescence reflected in their faces. We may feel guilt for our bad decisions. Some of us may relive some bad memories. We may feel unworthy—or even unable at times—to initiate our daughters into womanhood. And that's okay, because it's not about us. It's about what God will do *through* us. It's about what God has done *for* us.

I believe that one of the greatest spiritual callings on our lives as moms is to give away what we never received. Showing your daughter what it means to be a godly woman, even if no one ever did that for you, is an incredible gift to you both. Our girls have finely tuned emotional radars. If there's trouble under the surface in an area of our lives, they've probably already sensed it. We can't really hide much from them, can we? (Especially our cash!)

The areas you feel least confident about are the areas you will be most vulnerable in. You'll have plenty of time to prepare and pray over what to share, so you will be sharing details that are appropriate. You may even discover that sharing out of your own brokenness and emptiness enables you to heal. Giving away what we never received opens our hearts for a fresh outpouring of God's mercy and grace. God will heal you in the broken places as you offer your story to Him and prepare to share your heart with your daughter.

My prayer for you is that *Queen Esther's Secrets* gives you as many blessings as it does your daughter. I pray it releases your generation, and hers, to experience God in new ways and see His power break forth as never before in your family.

If you're struggling with unforgiveness and shame, it's time to put down the stones. Send the crowd of condemnation away. Jesus isn't afraid of your emptiness. He sent the crowd away, but He stayed. He wants to set you free and watch you walk in freedom.

Why such an emphasis on beauty treatments? What should I do if my daughter is a total tomboy or prefers books to beauty?

Esther's story begins when she is wrenched from her home life and forced into a harem, where she was valued and judged by one thing alone: her beauty. In our culture no other business has such a claim on women: The cosmetics and weight-loss industries together bring in about 100 billion dollars a year. *There is no bigger message our daughters receive from our culture than this: To be happy and valued, be beautiful—at any cost.* We may not live in a harem, but the pursuit of beauty saturates our culture every bit as much as it did Esther's.

I don't want a "harem culture" defining beauty for my girls. I believe there is a spiritual connection between beauty and women, and we honor God when we delight in how He's made us. Mothers have a unique chance to initiate their daughters into beauty and redefine it in a healthy, life-affirming way. Your daughter is entering the years when her worth is largely defined—by the world and many of her peers—by how she looks. You have the chance to define beauty with her. Little splurges and beauty treats are a rite of passage that only women can share, and they affirm that being a woman and feeling beautiful just as God designed us is a good thing. We can begin to shift the focus of beauty to something more than skin-deep. We can demonstrate to our daughters that being a woman is a delight, but the source of radiant beauty is the Creator of radiant beauty.

Think back to the Victorian Age. (I am not suggesting any of us are old enough to have lived through it!) In those days, no Christian dared talk publicly about sex. It was taboo. Now within a relatively short period of time, our culture has made a nightmare of it. Today, porn is mainstream, and Christians who oppose it are seen as fringe groups. The Christian community is desperately trying to assert our influence and moral authority.

I think the subject of beauty is facing a similar change. Christians sometimes feel squeamish about beauty, suspecting that making yourself physically beautiful is somehow less than spiritual. We primp, groom, and gloss before church, but rarely do we have a deliberate, deep conversation about why we do it. We're abandoning our opportunity to influence the next generation, and signs of this desertion are everywhere. Women and men are being influenced to change their ideal of beauty to match what they've seen in porn.[1] A lost world is redefining beauty for our daughters. We've got to step in, assert our influence and authority, and reclaim beauty as a godly, good gift that is defined by God—not an advertising campaign.

Queen Esther's Secrets will give you the opportunity to define beauty in *all* its forms, including words, actions, and spirit. You can decide what beauty treats to keep, which to alter, and which to trade out for another activity that may be more meaningful to you and your daughter. Remember, no one knows more about beauty than a Christian mom. The world has defined it as skin-deep, but we're too smart to stop there. We know what real beauty is, how to get it, and how to care for ourselves so that it shines out. We also know that being a woman and indulging in beauty treats just for women is a delight. We're going to pass along those secrets to our girls, and they, like Esther, may help save their generation.

What happens if I miss a month?
Pick up next month where you left off and continue. *Queen Esther's Secrets* is meant to bless you and your daughter. Do what you can, what you feel led to do, and enjoy your daughter.

What happens during our Esther Year meeting each month?
Queen Esther's Secrets follows a simple format:

- Beauty: Take your daughter for a beauty treat (and you can indulge, too!).

- Food: Afterward, find a quiet place to enjoy a good meal or dessert.
- Stories: Share the stories you've remembered as you read the discussion questions for the month.

The format is simple so that the focus can be on you and your girl. My goal in writing this book is to be an unobtrusive third party, such as a fabulous hotel concierge. My job is to set up the evening, but the time together is yours alone. You may want to buy a notebook for yourself and one for your daughter so that you can reflect on the deeper truths you've uncovered during your "Esther Year." Use the space to record your thoughts, dreams, and prayers.

How do I prepare my daughter for the Queen Esther's Secrets meeting each month?

I would suggest that your daughter begin your year together by reading the story of Esther. Then, before you have your Esther meeting, you can give your daughter a sneak peek of what will happen by printing out the online invitation or writing a note that communicates the following information:

1. We'll be getting together for our Esther Year time together on this date and time:
2. This month's beauty treat will be:
3. This month's story verse is:
4. So when we're together, we're going to be talking about:

You can keep the day and time a secret each month and surprise her in different ways by leaving a note in unexpected places. Have fun with it! What a memorable year this will be for your daughter, getting notes at unexpected times, and being whisked away for a little pampering and girl talk. If your daughter would like to keep each note, she can place it in her journal and later record her thoughts about the time together. It will be a treasured keepsake of her journey into womanhood.

Think about slipping her surprise note to her in some unexpected ways:

- Hide a note in her backpack or lunch.
- Tape a note to her mirror.
- Tuck it inside a candy bar.
- Wrap it around a flower with a ribbon and leave it on her pillow.

I've given you a format and structure that will help you make some precious memories and share your hard-won wisdom without being accused of nagging or preaching. I hope *Queen Esther's Secrets* builds strong bridges of intimacy that will help you both weather the stormy years of adolescence and adult independence. I'll be praying for you on your journey together, and if you have questions or comments, please contact me at:

QES@gingergarrett.com

One last note before you begin: Remember to spend time in prayer before your Esther time every month. What you are doing may be dressed up in a feminine, fun format, but the wisdom you'll be sharing—the lessons from God that you've lived out—is life-changing. It may be years before you understand the full impact of this year in both of your lives. Setting aside this time may be one of the wisest investments of time and money you've ever made. Pray for the right stories to share. Pray for your daughter's heart to be open and softened while she is pampered. Pray that this year will awaken in her a longing for wisdom that will stay with her all of her life.

Beauty

We honor God when we present ourselves, by faith, as beautiful.

KEY VERSE:
[King Xerxes ordered his men] to bring him Queen Vashti resplendent in her royal crown. He wanted to show off her beauty to the guests and officials. She was extremely good-looking. (Esther 1:11)

What Is Beauty?

When our story opens, we are treated to an inside look at the feast of Xerxes. Notice that the biblical account gives great details: what the pavement looked like, what the goblets were made of, even the color of the curtains. How odd it is, then, that the most beautiful woman in the land, Queen Vashti, is given absolutely no identifying description. Esther, who will become her successor, is likewise given no description.

In fact, the Bible *never* gives a physical description of the women it names as beautiful. We don't know if they were short, tall, heavy-set, or thin. The most descriptive passages of a beautiful woman, in Song of Songs, describe her hair as resembling "a flock of goats" and her neck like shields standing together. It's lovely poetry as we see the woman through her lover's eyes, but it doesn't describe her exact appearance.

The Bible is not short on other details: Consider how much

space is devoted to describing lineages, the exact measurements of Noah's ark, Solomon's temple, weights and measurements of flour and oil, and so on. Those are interesting, but why would God intentionally omit details of a subject that fascinates everyone? Men are held captive by beauty, and women long for it. Why would God be so silent about what it actually is? Perhaps it is because of our tendency to worship idols instead of Him.

Think back to the Ten Commandments: We are commanded to worship only God, never an idol. While Moses was receiving the Ten Commandments, the Israelites were making a golden calf to worship. It angered God that His people wanted to worship a visible idol instead of worshiping Him. When we try to articulate a specific standard of beauty—"beautiful is blonde and 36-24-36," for example—we come dangerously close to making an idol out of beauty and worshiping it instead of God. Beauty is a reflection of God's character and His artistic nature, but the more we focus on defining human beauty in human measurements, the more we're distracted from God.

I heard it put wisely once: It is wrong to define beauty by measurable standards, because beauty is the exclusive domain of God. God articulates what is beautiful, and we are both His canvas and His audience.

How Do I Know I'm Beautiful?

Seeing our own beauty begins when we're willing to see beauty in creation as an expression of God. When we stop judging His work by our standards, we begin to understand beauty in all its revelations:

- We're beautiful because we are filled with His beauty:

  Your vibrant beauty has gotten inside us—you've been so good to us!

  (PSALM 89:17)

- He has called us "marvelously made," an example of His "breathtaking" work:

  Oh yes, you shaped me first inside, then out;
      you formed me in my mother's womb.
  I thank you, High God—you're breathtaking!
      Body and soul, I am marvelously made!

  (PSALM 139:13-14)

- God is clearly smitten with us:

  The king is enthralled by your beauty;
      honor him, for he is your lord.

  (PSALM 45:11, NIV)

- Our beauty isn't dependent on exterior criteria that change with designers and seasons, but on what God has done within us and continues to do as we walk with Him:

  What matters is not your outer appearance—the styling of your hair, the jewelry you wear, the cut of your clothes—but your inner disposition.
      Cultivate inner beauty, the gentle, gracious kind that God delights in.

  (1 PETER 3:3-4)

God is beauty. God fills us with a radiance that transcends the exterior criteria the world tries to force upon us. God says you're beautiful, too, and encourages you to cultivate the beauty that delights Him. We honor God when we believe Him, so call yourself beautiful, by faith.

The Sacrifice of Beauty

Every time we define beauty as a specific look, we automatically exclude another woman. The era of worshiping blonde supermodels left African-American women feeling unlovely. The era of worshiping thin "twiggies" left curvy women feeling unlovely. The era of Marilyn Monroe left lithe women feeling unlovely. Every time we define beauty by our own standards, we hurt someone else. Defining beauty as a hair color, a measurement, or a weight also contradicts the main message of the gospel: Real love is sacrifice. The sacrifice you and I must make for our daughters' generation is refusing to define beauty and trusting God to reveal it. We show our trust in God when we:

- Believe what God says about beauty and our own loveliness
- Care for ourselves as good stewards of our bodies and appearances

A good steward sees to it that the best of care is given to what will someday be returned to its rightful owner. Our daughters will learn about stewardship from us, so we need to demonstrate it in our own lives. We can begin by attending to the way we are eating and making sure we feed ourselves as a loving Father would. We can exercise because it's freeing and energizing, not because it's a chance to get into a smaller size. We can fix what's broken or unhealthy without feeling self-conscious. If we have damaged skin or crooked teeth, there's nothing wrong with getting help fixing them. But when we cross the line and risk our health for a worldly standard that disrespects God, we have to ask if we're truly loving ourselves, our God, and our daughters.

We risk our health in a lot of ways: over-dieting, risky supplements, surgery, extreme worry, and anxiety over appearance. So I am going to ask this generation of moms to be ready to sacrifice to love the next generation. What lengths are you willing to go to in order to honor beauty as defined only by God and not our culture? Are you willing to sacrifice so that the next generation finds freedom? It might mean no more diets. It might mean canceling a magazine subscription that idealizes one body type and one type only. It might mean accepting your body as it is and saying no to cosmetic surgery.

Remember, every time you endorse a worldly standard of beauty, you exclude and hurt another woman, perhaps even your own daughter. You'll know it's a worldly standard if you can clearly define it, measure it, and believe that achieving it will somehow help you meet your goals. (*If only I looked like that, I could...*") We'll talk more about the power of sacrifice and how love always requires a sacrifice. For now, I want to challenge you to pray about the sacrifices you may need to make to enable your daughter to experience real beauty God's way.

Letting Go of Comparisons

Diversity in appearance is a sign that God is at work all over the world. We are made in His image, but each person reveals Him in a slightly different way. We honor God when we honor each other as beautiful without comparing ourselves. Comparing ourselves to others is forbidden in the Bible because it enslaves us and leads us into sin, temptation, and depression.

> "You shall not covet... anything that belongs to your neighbor."
>
> (EXODUS 20:17, NIV)

Comparing ourselves will destroy our faith. To compare is to ask God: "Did you give her more or less than me? Which of us did You take better care of? Which of us do You love more?" If another girl has the features we feel we lack, we take it as an indictment of God's love for us. Why would He give that feature to another girl and not to us? We get angry or depressed. We doubt His goodness, and eventually, we doubt Him. In Matthew 6:8, God reminds us:

> "Don't fall for that nonsense. This is your Father you are
> dealing with, and he knows better than you what you need."

When we compare and worry about what we don't have, we're questioning God's ability and intention to provide:

> You can be sure that God will take care of everything you
> need, his generosity exceeding even yours in the glory
> that pours from Jesus. Our God and Father abounds in
> glory that just pours out into eternity.
>
> (PHILIPPIANS 4:19-20)

God provides everything you need. Beauty can't. A world without God insists that beauty will bring love, fulfillment, self-acceptance, security, and friends. Without God, the world is desperate to chase beauty in the hopes of receiving these blessings. But you can ask for the blessings and receive them. You know the Source.

You can find the courage to let go of comparison when you realize that God will bless and prosper you and "give you what your heart desires" (Psalm 20:4). Making sure you are loved and blessed is God's responsibility. When we look to physical beauty to provide those things, we insult God's power and intention.

The pressure we feel to be beautiful in the world's eyes is the same pressure our daughters feel. Even if we haven't resolved the conflicting emotions we feel about our own beauty and appearance, we have years of experience that we can offer them. You don't have to be finished growing spiritually and emotionally in order to talk with your daughter about true beauty. It's enough that you take this time to let her know she's not alone. Tonight, have some laughs at the expense of the world's myths and enjoy yourself heartily. After all, the most beautiful woman in the room is usually the one laughing.

PREPARING FOR YOUR MEETING

This Month's Beauty Treat: skin-care lesson
Beauty begins by getting rid of impurities and rinsing away the unhealthy residue and pollution from the world

At:

Appointment date and time:

Where we'll eat:

Story Stirrers
1. Who were the most beautiful women to you when you were a young girl? How did you define beauty?

2. How do you define and measure beauty today? How has your understanding of beauty changed over time?

3. Since God said "beauty soon fades" (Proverbs 31:30), why do you think He made us beautiful?

4. What are the traps of pursuing beauty that you wish your daughter could avoid?

Go Back for Seconds

1. With a concordance, look up the verses in the Bible about beauty. Write down the common themes you see. How would you define beauty according to the Bible?

2. Both of you name the three most beautiful women you know. What is it that makes them beautiful—is it more than appearances?

PREPARE YOUR DAUGHTER
FOR THE ESTHER MEETING

1. We'll be getting together for our Esther Year time on this date and time:
2. This month's beauty treat will be: skin-care lesson.
3. This month's story verse is: Esther 1:11.
4. So when we're together, we're going to be talking about: beauty.

Community

Living in community prepares us to experience God's divine intervention in our story.

KEY VERSE:
It's not only the king Queen Vashti has insulted, it's all of us, leaders and people alike in every last one of King Xerxes' provinces. (Esther 1:16)

Our Story Begins as Another One Ends

Queen Vashti was thought to be the most beautiful woman in the kingdom of Persia, which was centered in the country now known as Iran. During a wildly extravagant party thrown by her husband, King Xerxes, she was asked to appear before her drunken husband so that he could show off her beauty to all the other men. (Some scholars think the king was specifically asking her to wear her crown—*and nothing else!*) She refused, and she did it in such a way that Xerxes was humiliated in front of all of his advisors and the men of his kingdom.

We can't judge Vashti too harshly. We don't have enough information to know whether her refusal was a rude snub or an entirely appropriate moral reaction. (Put yourself in her shoes: If your husband called you on his cell phone while on a fishing trip with his buddies and asked you to show up naked and bring brownies, how would you react?) If the "naked theory" is correct, she made the right choice not to appear—but even so, her refusal and the way she delivered it took its toll. The reverberations from her decision would soon be felt by every family in the kingdom, which extended across dozens of provinces.

Vashti lived in a community led by a king who ruled them all—a court of advisors who influenced his decisions and the subjects who had to obey him. No one could operate autonomously without affecting others. Vashti's story, which ends at the beginning of Esther's story, highlights for us a common narrative theme in all the stories of the Bible: the power of community. When we live in community, our actions impact many people. Our failures and conflicts give God an open door to do what He does best: redeem, transform, and set His people free. What a blessing, moms! Our failures in our own relationships are open doors for God to walk through and change our stories!

The Beginning of Community

The first story of community is, of course, Adam and Eve. I think it's interesting that Adam walked with God daily in the garden, and yet God said it wasn't good for Adam to be "alone." Technically, Adam wasn't alone, was he? He had God, face-to-face, every day. But God knew *community* would be the final touch on creation. When Eve was created, one of her purposes was to give Adam a community, a family to belong to. He would still walk with God daily (they both would), but something extraordinary was added in this new dimension. God was telling us it's not good enough to walk alone with Him; we have to walk with Him *and* hold hands with someone else. Perhaps we can only understand God as we share Him with another. Community in paradise was going to be a wonderful thing.

But whatever the God-blessed reasons for placing us immediately in community, it fell apart pretty quickly. One talking snake was all it took. In this perfect setting of paradise, one individual sinned and then enticed the other, who followed instead of standing up and fighting for the truth. And then the community changed. Children came into the picture, and Adam and Eve had a chance to live out community in a new context. Then one brother killed the other. Is it just me, or does it seem like this community thing just isn't working out? The biblical story just keeps expanding from there, and every turn of the page brings us new conflicts and fresh disputes.

What have we missed? We struggle to provide idyllic homes for our families, and often things end no better than they did in Eden. We expect community to bring us comfort and shelter us from temptation and disappointment, but sometimes it seems to do the opposite. Community, at least as far as I can see in the Bible, is intended to give us many godly graces, but it also causes us to confront the worst in ourselves and others.

So let's continue Esther Year with a careful examination of the myths, mysteries, and deep mercies of community.

What Is Community? How Does the Bible Define It?

The Bible has many references to families of origin, or birth families. God clearly acknowledges the family unit. The Bible also recognizes another family, calling the many believers in Christ a "body" of believers and a spiritual family. It's a family God has taken great care to create, calling each of us to be His child:

> Long, long ago he decided to adopt us into his family
> through Jesus Christ.
>
> (EPHESIANS 1:5)

We may have blown it in the Garden of Eden, but God's not done with this idea of community yet. He gives us a physical family as our first community, and then adopts us into the larger community of His own family when we become Christians. Marriage is another community we experience when we leave our families to create a new one. These communities overlap and insulate us, but because we are all interconnected, our actions have multiple reactions. When Xerxes banished Vashti, it affected men and women throughout his kingdom and set off a chain reaction of events.

God created these overlapping communities so that He could use them to accomplish His will through us. I think it's clear from the biblical accounts of community that God anticipated our failures. He knows we all fail to live up to the responsibilities of living in community, but He has a specific plan for our failures.

Failure to Thrive

Once upon a time, those words struck cold fear into every mother's heart. Failure to thrive meant a baby wasn't getting enough nourishment or was unable to flourish despite the mother's care. Thank God that now, failure to thrive in infants is a diagnosis, not a sentence. The phrase might well be forgotten by the time we hold our grandchildren.

However, "failure to thrive" is a wonderfully accurate description of God's plan for our growth as individuals in community. God uses our failures to help us to thrive. We all fail to live a perfect life full of love, but God uses these moments to teach us within the context of a healthy community. It's difficult to show each other unmerited grace and to treat each other as Christ treats us, but it's the way we begin to reap the rewards of community. Look at what He says in James 3:18:

> You can develop a healthy, robust community that lives
> right with God and enjoy its results *only* if you do the hard
> work of getting along with each other, treating each other
> with dignity and honor.

It's hard work to live in community, because people fail us. We fail ourselves. But when we do the "hard work" of loving and living in community anyway, despite the failures, weaknesses, and annoyances, we allow God to teach us who we are, and how to relate to each other.

Sometimes I wonder what's wrong with my daughters and me, because we butt heads so often. Just as we're settling down for a peaceful evening, one of them becomes the Bride of Frankenstein. My dad was watching us as a family recently and breathed a sigh of relief. "You're a good mom," he said, "*and* your kids fight all the time!" He had always assumed that I had fought with my brothers when we were growing up because of some fault of his. (It wasn't a fault of his. It was entirely my brother's.)

As parents, we often buy into the lie that: If I'm a good parent, everyone will get along. The truth is, once you clip that hospital bracelet off the baby and the baby figures out you can't do a return, life will get messy. And we'll soon look back with nostalgia to the days when the mess could be confined to a diaper!

Adam and Eve were the first to experience this frustrating cycle of community and conflict. After the Fall, they were disconnected from the Source of continuous peace and acceptance. They looked to each other to fill the aching void, but this only caused more conflict. One of my favorite authors, Anne Trippe, puts it this way:

> There was no option but to try to get by their performance and from each other what they had previously received so freely and unconditionally from God's life . . . But nothing they could devise worked to fill their longing to be restored to that former state of satisfaction and completeness.[1]

We can't force our families to work by our own power. That's because God intends to free us from the strategies we rely on to meet our needs—and our daughters' needs—apart from God. Eve first reached for the Tree of Knowledge attempting to meet her need without God. And God is still working on us all these years later, trying to get us to put down the fruit and trust Him. We develop little strategies to "help God help us." We try to keep everyone happy—thinking that this time around, life will be paradise and we won't feel the effects of sin. The bad news is, even our best-looking "strategies"—pleasing, promising, and pushing others—will fail. God wants each of us in the family to come to the end of ourselves so He can fill us with Himself:

"The strategies . . . can look good and be well-intentioned, but they prevent us from experiencing the good things the Lord has provided for us."[2]

We can't experience the robust life of community until we surrender our agendas and egos. That's what makes a community work—not the absence of conflict, but allowing the conflict to expose our self-centered strategies, asking God to help us walk free from them, and receiving abundant blessings in their place. Although community is guaranteed to bring us difficulty, it is designed to bless us. The conflict creates an opportunity for us to experience God's mercy. What a fabulous trade-off!

The Community of Family

God designed community to bring us comfort and encouragement, to give us a sense of history and belonging, and to give us tangible expressions of His great love for us. The community of the family is especially powerful stuff. Just ask my therapist. (I'm kidding, Mom!) Our daughters need us, and the power of this particular community shows up in the most unusual places:

Teens who eat dinner with their parents six or seven times a week are four times less likely to [smoke] cigarettes, three times less likely to smoke marijuana, and nearly half as likely to drink as those who eat dinner with their parents twice a week or less.[3]

Family gives your daughter a sense of comfort, stability, identity, acceptance, and belonging. Family soothes wounds from the world and dusts us off when we fall. Our larger community, the family of Christ, is designed to mirror these same qualities of protection and encouragement.

The Community of Mother and Daughter

"If it's not one thing, it's your mother." Community between mother and daughter has been the source of countless jokes and exasperations. The mother-daughter bond is both intimate and prone to conflict for so many reasons: Our daughters feel like an extension, and a reflection of us. We want to be proud of them and keep them from making our mistakes, but they want the independence to make their own decisions. Moms may not want to share their past, and daughters may not want to share everything going on in their present. Each of us is emotionally invested in how the other sees us. There can be an awful lot of eye rolling and sighing, and mothers and daughters can feel real guilt about the conflict.

Moms always ask the questions, "Am I raising her well? Am I doing this right?" We feel anxious that we're not enough or that we're too much of the wrong thing. Add onto this turbulent mix the fact that our daughters are coming into their own beauty and vitality just as we're noticing crow's feet and coming to grips with the realities of aging. We start to understand the answers just as our daughters are asking the questions. Because of our mistakes we want them to have better lives, but we don't want them to know what some of those mistakes were. Love raises the stakes. We care more about the other's opinion, their mistakes and bad decisions. All this love can make us unbearable to live with at times!

This is where and why the lessons we've learned about the purpose of community have such impact. When we understand that every conflict is used by God to release us from sinful attitudes and behaviors, it's just a tiny bit easier to bear it. God is using our human nature to show us His divine character. He intends to bless us right now, even in the middle of the eye rolling and door slamming.

It's not pleasant or easy, but we can entrust the mother-daughter bond to God because we know He is committed to both of us. As moms, it's humbling to accept that we are still learning and growing in obedience. How awesome that God is using our weakness to bless our daughters. We don't have to hide anything from Him! Everything we have, are, and were can be used by God to craft a brilliant future for our daughters.

Still, there's a lot we want to hide or pray our girls forget. We know we've failed. Sinned. Hurt others. Screamed. Ran red lights and drunk milk straight from the carton. We're not perfect, but we want nothing less than perfection for our girls. We're terrified that the number one obstacle to our girls' development may just be us. The number one question of moms is, "Am I enough?"

We're not, but God says *He* is. God promises His grace is enough to sustain us even though we feel the thorns of life:

> And then he told me,
> My grace is enough; it's all you need.
> My strength comes into its own in your weakness.
>
> Once I heard that, I was glad to let it happen. I quit
> focusing on the handicap and began appreciating the
> gift. It was a case of Christ's strength moving in on my
> weakness.
>
> (2 CORINTHIANS 12:9)

God will sustain our daughters, too, even when *we're* the thorns. God is going to bless us both, right in the middle of our failures and weaknesses. Your daughter needs to understand that the mark of a great relationship isn't necessarily how well the two of you get along, but what God is able to do in you when you don't get along. The relationship is designed to fail at exactly those points where we need to experience God.

Conflict in the community of family is not a reflection of our worth as mothers and daughters. You can encourage your daughter by sharing how community creates conflict so that God's power can work through her and free her of unhealthy self-reliance. Friends, peers, family, youth groups, and even us dear ol' moms will bring conflict and disappointment so that God can demonstrate His love for her in setting her free. The more she understands the role of conflict within her communities, the more she can weather the storms without accusing you of sending the rain.

PREPARING FOR YOUR MEETING

This Month's Beauty Treat: manicure

The muscles in the hands and fingers are so interconnected, you can't easily move one finger without moving others. But working in unison, a hand can create a masterpiece as glorious as the Sistine Chapel, or offer comfort as simple and sweet as cooling a fevered brow.

At:

Appointment date and time:

Where we'll eat:

Story Stirrers

1. What was the most difficult part of community living you experienced with your own family growing up? How did working through the conflict bless you and create a more godly character?

2. How have your communities changed as you moved through your teen years into adulthood and parenting? What were the hardest transitions?

3. How has the community of mother and daughter changed you as both a daughter and a mom?

Go Back for Seconds

1. What can you do with your daughter to give a sense of community to those who have none—the elderly and abandoned?

2. What communities is your daughter in? What challenges is she facing? How do you see God working in her through those difficulties?

PREPARE YOUR DAUGHTER
FOR THE ESTHER MEETING

1. We'll be getting together for our Esther Year time on this date and time:
2. This month's beauty treat will be: manicure.
3. This month's story verse is: Esther 1:16.
4. So when we're together, we're going to be talking about: community.

Emotions

Being a "good Christian" doesn't make us immune from being human.

KEY VERSE:
Let the king appoint officials in every province of his kingdom to bring
every beautiful young virgin to the palace complex of Susa. (Esther 2:3)

The size of Xerxes' harem was astronomical: hundreds, perhaps thousands, of girls brought to live together under one roof, all competing to win the affection of the king and become the queen. Perhaps Xerxes' harem provided the inspiration for the television show, *The Bachelor*.

Esther's year in the harem was a fast-forward puberty condensed into one year. Having grown up with her Uncle Mordecai (some translations refer to him as her cousin), she probably didn't know about the changes that would happen to her body or the ups and downs of emotions when she was plunged into a world of women, hormones, moods, and stress. Everyone's cycle was probably synchronized, too. The stress was unthinkable. Emotions were in an uproar. An entire kingdom and the right to be queen was on the line. The losers would be stuck in a wife's harem, never to return to society again. How did Esther survive all this with grace and go on to become a heroine of the faith? How can you help your daughter survive the emotional upheavals in her own life?

An interesting bit of research I did for this book was to compare headlines from three popular teen magazines and three popular women's magazines. Every headline was put in a category, such as health, relationships, and money. Every time a headline appeared in that category, I gave the category one point. (I took out the weight loss category below because teen magazines often have editorial policies that they will not run weight-loss articles in order to help fight the eating disorder epidemic.) The final breakdown of the top categories looked like this:

Women's Magazines

Health	5
Emotions	4
Recipes	3
Beauty	3

Teen Magazines

Life Stories	5
Relationships	5
Fashion	4
Emotions	3

There are radical differences of content between teen and women's magazines, but one topic received almost identical coverage in both groups: emotions. Obviously, women of every age are looking for information on handling moods, emotions, hormones, and stress.

Not so with our men, apparently. Just for fun I analyzed the headlines from popular men's magazines, and the hottest topic was fashion, as in, "How Women Want You to Dress." Other major topics were politics, sex, cars, and how to find a great steakhouse. There were absolutely no headlines on handling emotions!

What we *feel* is a complex equation from the inner processes of chemistry, biology, emotion, and thoughts. While every family is predisposed to certain patterns, each of us can learn to accept life's emotional roller coaster and trust God in the rough spots. Being Christians doesn't make us immune to stress and bad hormone days. Good information and a lot of reassurance from you, mom, is a great first step to diffusing your daughter's apprehension about the hormonal changes ahead.

This book won't cover the scientific details of hormonal changes at puberty. (You can find a list of helpful resources at the back of this book if you'd like to get more information for your daughter.) It will help you to prepare your daughter emotionally and mentally for the changes ahead. You'll also be able to talk with her about how you've learned to cope with any inherited issues such as depression.

As a mom, you have a unique opportunity to impact your daughter's health and emotional well-being. Listen to what Dr. Christiane Northrup has to say about her patients and the influence of their mothers:

A mother's often unconscious influence on her daughter's health is so profound that years ago I had to accept that my medical skills were only a drop in the bucket compared to the unexamined and ongoing influence of her mother. If a woman's relationship with her mother was supportive and healthy, and if her mother had given her positive messages about her female body and how to care for it, my job as a physician was easy. Her body, mind, and spirit were already programmed for optimal health and healing. If, on the other hand, her mother's influence was problematic, or if there was a history of neglect, abuse, alcoholism, or mental illness, then I knew that my best efforts would likely fall short.[1]

Never underestimate the lasting influence of a mom like you!

How Can I Prepare My Daughter for the Ups and Downs of Changing Hormones in the Teen Years?

You are already doing a great job, mom. How do I know that? You are leading your daughter through a meaningful initiation into womanhood. You are communicating to her that becoming a woman is a wonderful thing, even with all the ups and downs she'll experience. How we feel about the destination sets the tone for the journey. Remember that she'll likely hear horror stories from her friends about PMS, cramps, and hormonal swings. She may not be sure what to expect as she gets older, but you can bet she wouldn't get a balanced picture without you.

My grandmother did an exceptional job in this particular area. I could tell that she loved being a woman. She loved flutters of attraction when my grandfather was around, loved the way she was formed, loved the special privileges only women shared, like perfume and lotions. She communicated to me in a million little unspoken ways that being a woman was enjoyable. I couldn't wait to be a woman because I wanted to be like her. I am sure her perspective made adolescence easier for me. I didn't dread my period. I put up with hormone swings and cramps because of the mystery and delight of finally achieving what seemed so special.

Mom, you've probably already prepared your daughter very well, just by enjoying the life God has blessed you with. The more stories you can share about the joys of being a woman, the better equipped she'll be for the difficult times being a woman creates. What an incredible gift you're giving your daughter this year!

How Does Family History Contribute to Emotional Patterns?

If there are stressful or particular familial patterns, this is a great time to discuss them. If there is a family history of depression or anxiety, it would be helpful for your daughter to know in advance what that feels like and what behaviors may signal a need for a medical evaluation. This isn't a frilly feminine conversation, but it's important. The more your daughter understands her family history, the better equipped she'll be to cope. It was a blessing to me that I could talk about my moods and emotions with my mom and grandmom. They always told me what they had experienced so that I knew what to expect. Sometimes just knowing that it's normal to struggle with a particular issue helps us get through it gracefully. It alleviates the need to keep our struggles secrets and frees us from shame and fear.

Of course, if the issue has a medical component, you'll need professional help. If the issue is spiritually based, you and your daughter are perfectly poised this year to confront it, pray about it, and banish that snake from the family "garden."

How Does Stress Affect a Woman Differently from a Man?

Under stress, it's not uncommon for women to seek out someone or something to nurture. That's why we get baby pangs at the most inopportune stages of life, or feel compelled to buy a pet on a whim. Women feel drawn to nurture others because it's as soothing as being nurtured ourselves. I am especially guilty of this. When I'm stressed out, my husband knows where to find me: in the computer room, looking wistfully at websites of Saint Bernard dogs to adopt. He calls this "bernardgraphy," and reminds me I don't have room for a third dog. Another friend of mine begs her kids to let her hold them like infants, just one more time. I believe there is a great deal of exasperated eye rolling going on in that house.

If we can't find something to nurture, we often head to the kitchen. Chocolate is the number one drug of choice for the stressed-out female, followed closely by ice cream. A few of us will deviate and head for the pantry to dig out a bag of chips. There are good reasons—and solid science—behind each choice. Many of these foods stimulate the release of "feel-good" chemicals in the brain.

Thankfully, chocolate, especially the darkest variety, is packed with antioxidants and is actually pretty good for your body. The rest of the junk food—well, I think we both know it's not good for our health or weight. But you may have to wait to tell me that until I put down my ice-cream spoon.

Stress and Prayer

Jesus gave us a no-calorie alternative to handling life's stresses. He encouraged us to pray:

> "Embrace this God-life. Really embrace it, and nothing
> will be too much for you. This mountain, for instance:
> Just say, 'Go jump in the lake'—no shuffling or shilly-
> shallying—and it's as good as done. That's why I urge you
> to pray for absolutely everything, ranging from small to
> large. Include everything as you embrace this God-life,
> and you'll get God's everything."

(MARK 11:22-24)

Jesus knew that prayer changes things—especially us. Some types of prayers are frantic whispers; others are deep meditations on God's Word and listening for His voice. This type of prayer may actually change the way our brains are wired. A study on meditation showed that quiet meditation produces changes in the area of the brain responsible for our emotions. Among those who practiced quiet meditation, this area of the brain showed a significant increase in activity, and the study participants also showed an increased immune response. In other words, they were better able to process emotions and fight illness. The results were still present four months after the study concluded.[2]

Prayer is an extremely effective way to manage emotional ups and downs, because it grounds us in the reality of our faith, releases our negative emotions, and may even boost our brain's ability to process the situation.

What Strategies Help Manage Emotions and Stress?

Three other practical solutions to encourage your daughter in are:

1. Regular exercise
2. Adequate sleep
3. Healthy diet

Most of us know these are important, but we don't rigorously practice them. I am certainly guilty of this. But in the teen years, which are so pressurized, we just can't underestimate how valuable the simplest solutions are. Your girl may be pushing herself in school and activities and getting to bed too late, or using sugar and caffeine to keep herself artificially alert. To make matters worse, the culture tells girls that the only purpose of exercise is to lose weight. However, exercising releases stress and encourages a stable mood like no wonder drug on earth. In fact, women who exercise may experience less depression and anxiety during their menstrual cycle.[3] Moms, we can encourage by example: exercising daily to relieve our stress and not checking the scale to see if it's "working."

Sleep is another of God's blessings to improve mood and cope with stress, but it can be interrupted if we focus on our negative emotions. Those of us who can practice "setting aside" our emotions at night experience better sleep.[4] To help your daughter do this, you may want to buy her a nighttime devotional and journal. I believe what we read just before sleep has an impact on how well we sleep. Challenge your daughter to use the time right before she goes to bed to "give everything away" on paper, release the events and emotions of the day, and reflect on one last uplifting thought. This will help her enjoy the deep sleep her body—and her emotions—need.

How Can I Protect My Daughter Emotionally?

Suzanne Eller, a writer who specializes in teen issues, had this to say recently about parents and teens: "Most parents are worried about violence, but the real violence in a teen's world is personal violence— self injury, depression, suicide."

A mom's vigilant love is a powerful defense against this type of violence. A mom who is connected to her teen, listening and sharing, has the greatest chance of protecting her daughter from self-damage and the violence of a culture set against her growth as a daughter of God. The time you spend leading your daughter through *Queen Esther's Secrets* won't shelter her from feeling rocky emotions, but it will help her heal from the jagged nips and scrapes life inflicts on all of us. And that's a bonus I'll take any day over finding a great steakhouse!

PREPARING FOR YOUR MEETING

This Month's Beauty Treat: makeup lesson

Now that her skin is well cared for, tasteful cosmetics can accent what is lovely. So often cosmetics are overdone because they try to mask or hide features. A makeup application is a great visualization of emotion management: learning to highlight the good and focus on it without masking or hiding the real self.

At:

Appointment date and time:

Where we'll eat:

Story Stirrers

1. Did you have a difficult time in adolescence with hormonal changes and mood swings? How did you cope, and did it help? Are there secrets and tips you can share with your daughter?

2. What seems more real and urgent to you: your emotions, or the truth of God's Word? Why is it hard for us as women to let go of what we feel and put our trust in what is true?

3. How has prayer and faith in God changed your outlook and ability to handle life's ups and downs?

Go Back for Seconds

1. Buy your daughter a nighttime devotional and a bedside journal. Buy one for yourself, too. Commit to write one page a night and read one page a night, every night, until the next *Queen Esther's Secrets* meeting. Do you notice a significant change in sleep quality and emotion management?

2. Buy a CD of Christian meditation music and swap it out for noisier CDs. I like ones that offer hymns or Scripture set to quiet background music. I listen to mine in the morning while

getting ready and again while cooking dinner. Those two times are key to set my mood and soothe my nerves—what are your most important times and what can you listen to?

PREPARE YOUR DAUGHTER
FOR THE ESTHER MEETING

1. We'll be getting together for our Esther Year time on this date and time:
2. This month's beauty treat will be: makeup application lesson.
3. This month's story verse is: Esther 2:3.
4. So when we're together, we're going to be talking about: emotions.

Friendships

Friends shape us effortlessly, but a good friendship takes effort to shape . . . and shapes the world around us.

KEY VERSES:
Hegai . . . assigned her seven personal maids from the palace, and put her and her maids in the best rooms in the harem. (Esther 2:9)

Every day Mordecai strolled beside the court of the harem to find out how Esther was and get news of what she was doing. (Esther 2:11)

Your daughter's community of peers has a far-reaching effect on her life. Consider these equations: Her peer group is determined largely by her choice of activities, and these activities influence which college she applies to, and her degree influences what she does for a living. Her peer group influences who she dates, and who she dates determines who she'll marry. Her peer group influences her values, and her values determine her lifestyle.

Girls form communities with their peers from a very early age. We are social creatures and enjoy the bonds of community. As a mom, you don't have to stand outside of the community like Mordecai, pacing back and forth every day hoping to catch a glimpse of her life on the inside. You can actually help steer her into community by helping her choose what activities she'll participate in. Let me explain a bit:

Anecdotal evidence suggests the power of a group is more important than individual friendships. If two girls are friends but one joins a new group the other friend isn't involved with, the friendship is probably doomed. Adults don't experience this as much because we can compartmentalize better than preteens. I have friends who are professional writers, friends who never read, friends who are health nuts, and friends who pose as "candy fairies" and leave sugary sweets in my mailbox. Women understand that we are different people in every relationship: mothers, daughters, friends, and wives. Being friends with someone who is different doesn't shift us off-center because we are used to changing hats effortlessly.

Preteens are much more rigid in their interpretation of themselves and the world around them. So while individual friendships may flourish for a season, it's the life of the group that allows a friendship to flourish or wither away. This is your secret weapon, mom: focusing on a positive peer group to steer her toward. We can observe who is involved in which activities and steer her toward activities that attract the healthiest peers. Like Mordecai, we would love to be able to see more, shelter more, and steer more, but our girls are so often out of our sight and reach. Friendship, especially friendships in community, wields its power as we watch. Because we can help choose which activities she spends her time on, we have a strong hand in picking her peer group. Her activities will determine her group, and her group will determine who her closest friends are.

This will hopefully relieve you of a little pressure. It can be a struggle to know which way to direct your child. Should she focus on art or math? Is she good enough to be on the soccer team and get a scholarship, or will she always regret missing a chance to be on the newspaper staff at school?

It's more important that she devote herself to the activities that will bring the right *people* into her life, rather than struggling to find the "right *thing*" she is most talented at. Don't feel pressure to find her unique gift and push her in that direction. I suspect *who* she is involved with will have longer consequences than *what* she is involved with. You can illustrate it by this point. Suppose you spend the summer at a soccer camp with three of your best friends. At the end of the summer, do you unconsciously make kicking motions with your feet all the time? Do you block invisible goals while you talk? Nope. Soccer was just what you *did*. But think about how you talk, the words you use, your facial expressions and hand gestures. Unconsciously, you will mirror your friends. Soccer was what you *did*; your friends became who you *are*.

Take a long look at the groups that form around any one activity and use this as a decisive factor in how to steer your daughter. Those kids will become her closest friends. Moms who are part of vibrant Christian churches reap the blessing of having communities ready-made and waiting for their girls. Are there examples from your own life about the power of friendships, especially friendships formed in a community? You'll want to share these with your daughter later.

I can clearly trace a huge chunk of my adult life back to a decision I made in the eighth grade. I enrolled in a drama class. I didn't care about theater, but I really liked the people I met there. The next nine years were consumed by theater, as I went from awkward high school freshman to college senior on a theater scholarship. My friendships with the other girls anchored me through some turbulent teen weather. I thank God that almost every one of my theater friends was level-headed, intelligent, and given to making wise decisions. That one decision of which activity to be a part of shaped my personality, influenced my choice of colleges and majors, and also influenced who I dated and what my social boundaries were.

Changes to Expect in the Teen Years

"Some friendships are only for a season," my mom told me when I was young. When a friend began to shift her interests or time, and

I sensed we were drifting apart, it was a little easier to bear because my mom had set my expectations from the outset. What can you do to help prepare your daughter for the changes in her friendships that are coming?

The teen years are so turbulent. Peer groups change, girls will divide into new groups as their interests change, and choices of colleges will begin to separate friends. Even dating changes friendships: Some girls will get so wrapped up in a boyfriend that they will all but drop their other friends. These turbulent years continue right into the single years. Marriage disrupts tight friends and women have to renegotiate friendship all over again, and then babies come along and divide friends again into mommies and not-quite-ready-yets. It wasn't until I was several years and several kids into my marriage that I felt my friendships were settling down into a comfortable, dependable circle.

As moms, we set expectations and model friendships. We still face disruptions occasionally, but these difficult moments can be great teaching opportunities. When friends move, divorce, are widowed, or experience a major life event, the relationship changes. We can demonstrate to our girls how to reach out and when to let go. We can encourage them that change is a healthy and normal, but sometimes painful, part of friendship. Our girls can expect disruptions and disappointments as they form friendships, but this is not a reflection of their social standing or skills. Like a flower in bloom, each petal has to peel away to claim its own bit of sun.

What We Owe Our Friends

A national poll showed that girls are fearful of being influenced or coerced into doing something they know is wrong. We've done a good job of warning teens about the dangers of peer pressure that society often looks at in a negative light. However, peer pressure can also be a good thing. How many times have you ordered a salad at lunch because your friend did, when you could have just as easily ordered a deep-fried plate of cheese fries? How many times have you been extra careful about what you wore or said because of your respect for the person you were with?

God promises us that a godly friend will challenge us and bring out the best in us.

> You use steel to sharpen steel, and one friend sharpens another.
>
> (PROVERBS 27:17)

The power of a group of godly friends can encourage everyone to stay on course. Positive peer pressure can shield us from unnecessary temptation because we feel a responsibility to uphold a group's values.

How Can I Help My Daughter Influence Her Friends?

As moms, we know we can't control what our daughters say or do when they're with their friends. But we can love. The more we love our girls, the more we communicate acceptance. The more we affirm and encourage our daughters, the better they will be at influencing the world around them. I first noticed this phenomenon when I was in junior high. I could tell who had loving parents and who went home to war zones. Girls who were deeply loved didn't need as much approval or affirmation from their peers, and so they weren't afraid to say no to unhealthy and destructive behaviors. Love had given them a steel core of inner strength. And secretly, even the bad girls wanted more of what they had.

So love your girl, and be aware that the more you love her, the more those who aren't as deeply loved will be drawn to her. Unloved girls lash out or latch on. Your daughter will attract one or both of those reactions, and she should be prepared. You'll have a chance to walk her through forgiveness and patience and encourage her to bring those girls closer into the loving community and the love of God they need. If you're plugged into a vibrant church community, this is a natural opportunity to include a girl who needs to be loved.

Loving your daughter makes her influential, because loved people make decisions differently. As you love your daughter through all her ups and downs, you're illustrating how to love people even when it's difficult. Your daughter will be able to model love to others and point some desperate, thirsty girls to the Living Water of God.

I hope this is an encouragement to you. Your hard work is never in vain. By loving your daughter, you'll have the opportunity to influence a world of people you may never meet.

PREPARING FOR YOUR MEETING

This Month's Beauty Treat: haircut

Treat your daughter to an expert hairdresser who can create a new look for her, or just freshen the cut she already loves. Hairstyles can change many times as a girl discovers her identity—and so can friendships. A great cut—and a great friend—always bring out her best.

At:

Appointment date and time:

Where we'll eat:

Story Stirrers

1. What activities were you a part of in school, and how did the friendships you formed there impact your life?

2. How did friendships keep you on track or steer you off course?

3. What do you wish you had known then about friendships and the influencing power of a group?

4. Were there girls you were able to influence? How were their lives impacted?

Go Back for Seconds

1. Pray about extending your circle of friendships by offering hospitality to someone new. Is there a new family in the neighborhood? A new coworker?

2. Who are the friends who have shaped your life the most? Send them thank-you cards and express your appreciation.

PREPARE YOUR DAUGHTER
FOR THE ESTHER MEETING

1. We'll be getting together for our Esther Year time on this date and time:

2. This month's beauty treat will be: haircut.

3. This month's story verses are Esther 2:9,11.

4. So when we're together, we're going to be talking about: friendship.

Body Image

Accepting our bodies and embracing their purpose allows us to trust God with our lives.

KEY VERSES:
[Esther] had a good figure and a beautiful face. (Esther 2:7)

Right off he started her beauty treatments, ordered special food.
(Esther 2:9)

We've already talked about beauty. Is body image so different? In some ways, no. The lessons we learned about beauty also apply to body image:

- Beauty cannot be defined by the world's terms because it is not of this world. Beauty is from God, and He defines it.
- When we compare ourselves to others, we are not trusting God.
- Love calls us to sacrifice: to sacrifice our need to be better than others and to sacrifice our need to be defined as beautiful if it excludes someone else.

Our focus on body image includes these lessons but goes further and in different directions. How we feel about our bodies goes beyond our thoughts about our appearance. We develop our body image by how we feel about our body's *purpose* in addition to its design.

Hips, breasts, curves, and periods all remind us that the female body is unique because of its childbearing potential. Fertility and childbirth is a basic purpose of the design of our bodies. (It's not the only purpose, but it is a major one.) Society has changing views of the value of this purpose. These views cycle in and out of vogue and are dependent on economic factors, too. In cultures dependent on working the land, fertility and childbirth are prized. In Western culture, fertility and childbirth have fallen into disfavor. Childbirth is often seen as a disruption in career and pleasure, even when the child is wanted. How you feel about your fertility and your potential for childbirth will change the way you feel about your feminine design.

The Birth of Diets

In Esther's story, did you notice that she was supplied with special foods? She went on a diet of sorts, although Esther's diet was probably designed to fatten her up and increase her fertility. If Esther had a child, she could improve her position in the king's harem. Having bigger hips, breasts, and tummy rolls was a good thing. We've probably all heard of anorexics or athletes who lost their periods because their body fat dipped too low, but Esther's extra weight was meant to protect her body's fertility. In Esther's culture, the relationship between weight, body, and fertility was:

Feminine = Fat = Fertile = Desirable outcome

The birth of diets began as an explicit rejection of traditional Christian values. In the early 1900s when women were fighting for the vote, "flapper chic" came into vogue. No longer were fertile, feminine bodies prized. Young flappers rebelled against the Victorian culture and rejected traditional Christian values as well.

America's young women rushed to emulate the flapper aesthetic. They flattened their chests with tight bands of cloth in order to look as young and boyish as possible. But flapperhood was more than mere fashion. To an older generation of Americans the flapper symbolized a "revolution in manners and morals."[1]

The flapper's equation of body and weight went like this:

Thin = Freedom from restrictive morals = Desirable outcome

The birth of the American diet was not rooted in a love for God and our unique bodies. It was a rejection of those values, and women today are still paying the price.

It's important to understand the moral forces driving the ideal body image. When we critically examine the hidden messages of our culture, we can escape the pressure to conform. Ask *where* and *why*. *Where* did this ideal come from? *Why* is it desirable? Root out the truth. Pursue God and live out what He reveals to you, and "then you will experience for yourselves the truth, and the truth will free you."

Today, there is a growing influence on body image from the porn industry. An MSN/Elle poll showed that a significant number of people who watched porn said it changed their perception of the ideal female form. Porn is a perverted exaggeration of sexuality, and the female bodies in the films are often perverted and exaggerated through extreme surgery. Porn was once confined to seedy roadside stops and magazines kept under the counter. Today, porn is mainstream and becoming increasingly trendy and popular. As moms, we're hyper-aware of this; we spend a lot of time trying to protect our children from seeing it on their computers, phones, and television. If you begin examining the ideal female form espoused in the media, you'll begin to see how porn is changing the standard.

Moms who want to stand strong in a cultural free fall might discover that the first battle is not waged in a senator's office or by a boycott and petition. The first battle is accepting our body as it was designed, with all its implications, and refusing to be influenced by ungodly cultural ideals. Accepting your body is courageous, and Esther's story proves that the courage of one woman is enough to sway history.

Dr. Linda Mintle, a national expert on women's body image issues, encourages moms in "Making Peace with Your Thighs" in her book. She also offers a few tips for us as moms of preteen girls:

1. Educate yourself on what's normal during adolescence. Dr. Linda says, "a number of mothers brought their preteen daughters to me in order for me to evaluate them for an eating disorder. They didn't understand that the prepubescent plumpness they were seeing wasn't a weight problem but preparation for puberty changes. On the other hand are moms who see the signs and warnings of body obsession and ignore it."

2. Stress health and fitness over weight. Don't put her on a diet and don't allow her to talk such nonsense.

3. Don't become the food police. Instead, help her to grow into her weight by eating healthy and making good choices.

Defining Your Body

I have always had strong hands with long fingers and pronounced veins and muscles. They don't look anything like the lovely hands I see in lotion ads, smooth and sleek as they reach for the new product. I'm aware that my hands aren't beautiful in the world's standards, but I really love them anyway. Why? Because my mother once told me I had an artist's hands. Defining their purpose as something wonderful made their appearance unimportant.

How we feel about the purpose of our bodies unlocks the door to self-acceptance. Here are two other real-world examples:

- You can call a girl flat-chested or say she has a dancer's body.
- You can call a girl unfeminine or say she has an athletic build.

I've heard women define their big hips as "good for birthin' babies." It puts a good spin on a body that the world called unlovely. What messages can you give yourself and your daughter about the purpose of your bodies? Is there a particular feature that is troublesome? What can you tell yourself about the feature that will change how you feel about it?

The Curse

Naming an object changes how we feel about it. If you call yourself lithe, you'll feel better than calling yourself scrawny. If you call yourself voluptuous, you'll feel better than calling yourself pudgy. If you describe yourself as lovely, you'll feel lovely. You'll project that same warmth to the world around you. You reveal your inner life by your words. Words reveal how we think, and how we think reveals who we are:

> For as he thinks within himself, so he is.
>
> (PROVERBS 23:7, NASB)

The power of a name extends to all aspects of our bodies. How do you refer to the menstrual cycle? Is it The Curse? We need to find new names for our bodies and cycle if we want our daughters to feel good about having them. (I like the online nickname: AF or Aunt Flo. A visit from Aunt Flo certainly sounds better than a curse.)

In fact, some moms choose to celebrate the first arrival of AF with their daughters. It affirms that becoming a woman is a good thing—and our bodies are good, too. My mom was much too bashful to throw a period party, so I helped her out when I was about thirteen and got my first period. I marched into the living room, threw my arms in the air, and announced to my family, "Tonight, I am a woman." I had a talent for theatrics, but celebrating the moment still made me feel special. I never wanted to say I had been cursed.

Another habit we have is lamenting out loud that girls menstruate earlier than previous generations. We say it's because of the hormones in dairy products, and we worry out loud that there's something wrong with our girls' bodies and their periods. I confess to exactly all that. If you do, too, then you'll be relieved to read this quote from an expert on American girlhood, Professor Joan Jacobs Brumberg at Cornell University:

> In certain environments—including many societies in the past and some poor countries today—malnutrition and disease inhibit regular menarche and menstrual periods. Young women begin to menstruate early only where living conditions generate better diets and a decline in infectious diseases.[2]

There's nothing wrong with our girls' bodies. They are simply reaping the benefits our ancestors fought to give them: health, longevity, and strength. "Early" menstruation is not a sign that something is wrong with our daughters' bodies. It's a sign that everything's right.

Accepting Change

Moms, we all know our bodies have changed. These days, everything on my body has fled south and is fighting extradition! From childhood to teens and twenties, to childbirth and beyond, our bodies are designed to change as our lives do. Our weight fluctuates with our cycle every month, and hormones change our metabolism over the years. In the teen years this transformation is especially pronounced.

The changes are awkward: A girl's body changes from the outside working in. The outer bones lengthen first: hands and feet, then shin bones and forearms. Then her hips will widen, and she'll grow taller as her spine lengthens. A girl at a healthy weight can expect her weight to double as she moves from a ten-year-old girl to a young woman of eighteen. Her body is experiencing a dramatic change exactly at the moment that maintaining a perfect appearance is socially critical.

Because there is so much pressure to be perfect, our daughters are often mortified by these changes. It's like trying to do high tea on a raft in the ocean. We're supposed to flow with the rolling action, but instead we fight it and wonder why our tea party falls apart. We vow to master the ocean and try again.

Accepting our bodies can release some of this stress. If you accept the changes happening to your body—your metabolism, wrinkles, and hormones—you'll help your daughter weather the ongoing transformation of her body.

Plastic Surgery

Plastic surgery among teens is growing. A rite of passage to adulthood was once the keys to the car or receiving your period. Now, in some circles, the defining rite of passage is getting your first plastic surgery. When should a mom agree to surgery or decline it for herself or her daughter? I believe it comes down to a question of motivation. Motivation for teen cosmetic surgery breaks down as:

- Wanting more attention for your looks
- Wanting less attention for your looks

Some women and girls want surgery to get more attention. They want to be considered more beautiful and shapely in the eyes of the world so they will receive the attention they crave. If our daughters believed that they were inherently valuable, their interest in surgery might evaporate. The Bible promises us that "God will meet all your needs according to his glorious riches in Christ Jesus" (Philippians 4:19, NIV). You cannot be a good steward if you subject your body to surgery for the sake of attempting to secure for yourself what God has already promised. In these cases, it's my belief that surgery is not in God's will.

But some want surgery to avoid attention. If a woman or girl has a pronounced feature that continually invites unwarranted comments, looks, leers, and jeers, she's not asking for surgery because of vanity and a doubt God will provide. The pain she's experienced has probably driven her to God over and over. She's just anxious to be free of the effects of a fallen world: the mocking, taunting, and stigma of being different. Sometimes the most merciful thing we can do when there is a serious issue is let her talk to a surgeon who can explain what can be done and at what age. We can open the door on a painful conversation about self-worth and humiliation. Sometimes just knowing we've heard her and haven't dismissed the pain she's feeling can start a healing process and help her get through the roughest years.

No matter what we decide, God loves us and will continue to provide, nurture, and encourage us to grow in character and His will. We can model that for each other as we refuse to judge our sisters and continue to honor our own bodies as gifts from God.

PREPARING FOR YOUR MEETING

This Month's Beauty Treat: body pampering

Go shopping together and test lotions and powders. Splurge on a lotion that smells great and keeps skin moisturized. Buy a beautiful dispenser to keep it in, exclusively for her use.

At:

Appointment date and time:

Where we'll eat:

Story Stirrers

1. How do you feel about your body shape and size? What are the roots of these feelings?

2. How have body ideals changed since you were a teen? How have your own ideals changed?

3. What is the craziest thing you've ever done to get the "perfect" figure? Are there stories of what your mothers and grandmothers used to try?

4. Who prepared you for menstruation and how your body would change—or were you unprepared?

Go Back for Seconds

1. With your daughter, buy magazines from different sources: beauty, sports, parenting, homemaking. Cut out images of women's bodies and identify the underlying messages. Rate the message and the ad. Is the message appropriate and healthy? Is the ad effective at creating a desire to obtain that image?

2. Write down ten things you both like about your bodies.

3. Name a goal you have for your body, such as running a 10K race or participating in a physically challenging mission trip.

PREPARE YOUR DAUGHTER FOR THE ESTHER MEETING

1. We'll be getting together for our Esther Year time on this date and time:
2. This month's beauty treat will be: body lotions and powder. Pampering the body feels good and helps us feel good about our bodies.
3. This month's story verses are: Esther 2:7,9.
4. So when we're together, we're going to be talking about: body image.

Money

Let people see you, not your stuff.

KEY VERSE:
When it was Esther's turn to go to the king . . . she asked for nothing
other than what Hegai, the king's eunuch in charge of the harem, had
recommended. Esther, just as she was, won the admiration of everyone
who saw her. (Esther 2:15)

Why Is Finance Important? Why on Earth Does It Belong in a Rite-of-Passage Book?

Women try to find their identity in their looks, but we also find identity in how we spend our money. Credit card debt is at an all-time high, and families are saving less than they did during the Depression. Financial foolishness is a major cause of stress and the number-one reason cited for divorce. If you want to protect your marriage, enrich your spiritual life, know God's character and provision, and protect your daughter from lifelong consequences, finances are an essential topic.

Financial expert Ellie Kay, author of *The Debt Diet*, sums up the potential that moms have to teach their daughters about money:

Teaching her about money is the very best thing you can do
for her relationships. Moms may avoid talking about money
if they don't know much about it themselves, or don't want
to burden their daughter with financial worries. But financial

illiteracy among teens is at an all-time high, at the same time that teen spending power is at an all-time high.

Esther's story is not silent on finances. Esther was a smart financial cookie because she was grounded in her faith in God. Let me explain: As girls were brought to Xerxes for his consideration, they also brought a gift for him. It's likely that some girls brought gifts from their home provinces, elaborate and expensive tributes to build up Xerxes' ego and perhaps win his affection and become queen. If a girl had a chance to marry the ruler of such a powerful empire, this would be motivation to supply her with the best gift. I imagine that competition between the girls and their gifts was fierce, with the girls' parents and hometowns even contributing an offering. But Esther apparently only asked her caregiver Hegai what to take, and it probably wasn't much. She went to Xerxes just as she was, without exaggerated gifts and showy flashes of wealth. She had faith that God would do for her what wealth could not. Her actions suggest that she knew she was enough as she was.

Esther's challenge to us is to rely on God, not wealth. He can elevate us to positions of power and esteem without brand names, platinum cards, and cool cars.

Spending to Gain Identity

Having the newest, hottest, most expensive items makes us look rich. But as the old saying goes, "You can't spend yourself rich." Riches and honor come from God alone:

> To you, O GOD belong the greatness and the might,
>   the glory, the victory, the majesty, the splendor;
> Yes! Everything in heaven, everything on earth;
>   the kingdom all yours! You've raised yourself high
>   over all.

Riches and glory come from you,
>   you're ruler over all;
You hold strength and power in the palm of your hand
>   to build up and strengthen all.

>   (1 CHRONICLES 29:11-12)

Being a wise spender and saver shows God that you take His gifts seriously. But often, we only feel as desirable as the labels we own. How can we separate our identity from our labels? The first step is to open our eyes to what a label costs. Ellie Kay has an excellent suggestion for moms, which she uses with her own seven children. As a mom, you can offer to buy the item, but let the child buy the brand. If a pair of good tennis shoes without an exciting brand costs $40, give your child $40 for tennis shoes. If they want a brand-name pair that costs $140, they have to come up with the extra $100. Seeing in literal terms how much is wasted on brand names that add no value or life to the product will help lessen the attraction.

The second step is following in Esther's footsteps and being brave enough to face any situation without fancy gifts and goods.

Budgets

Do you have a budget? Do you know what you spend every month? At first, working through a budget was as pleasant as snorting powdered laundry detergent. I hated every moment. It felt insulting to put on paper every cent I spent and limit myself in some areas. I also switched to an all-cash system. I take out a small amount of cash every few days and can spend only that money. When it runs out, I stay home! (Just kidding. QVC, anyone?)

Those financial changes were unpleasant and hard to get used to. But the fabulous rewards overshadow the discomfort:

- The temptation to overspend is diminished. I have to make my cash last.
- Paying cash instead of charging makes me more aware of the value of money. I feel more like a mature adult. (Don't tell my kids I ever feel otherwise.)
- I don't feel sick when I get a credit card bill in the mail. (And yes, I do still have credit cards—who could ever give up the convenience of paying at the gas pump?)
- I feel hopeful about the future.
- There are no arguments about spending with my husband. We spend the agreed-upon amount and that's it. Tension is defused. The budget is an impersonal judge. It can't hear me whine.

You don't have to wait until you are a model of financial perfection to begin teaching your daughter about finances. Our relationships with our daughters grow and deepen as we work through our humanity together. We don't wait to become parents until we're spiritually and emotionally perfected, right?

A brilliant first step to take in teaching your daughter about money is helping her to set up a budget. You can give her a budget for school supplies, school lunches and snacks, clothes, or activities. Let her control what she spends, but there has to be a firm end to the money. When it's gone, it's gone. (As opposed to my former way of spending: "No cash? It's time to flash!" Visa, that is.) We all spend money very differently when it's our own. Having control *and* responsibility forces a girl to make wise choices or face the consequences. Experiencing small consequences now is a loving way to protect her from the ugly consequences in adulthood.

Some financial experts recommend giving your daughter a prepaid credit card or gift card. You may choose a cash system. But Ellie's got the icing on the cake to really motivate smart spending:

Let your girl keep the change. If she's got a budget for $100 for school supplies and she shops wisely and spends $85, she can pocket the difference. The caveat to this system is that all necessary items have to be accounted for. She can't avoid buying a winter coat or shoes to fit her growing feet just so she can keep the money.

Blessings Ahead

God has a lot to say about money, much more than other subjects. The Bible talks about money more than prayer! God knows that how we handle money has eternal impact on the world and ourselves. Throughout the Bible, God warns us about the misuse of money:

> A greedy and grasping person destroys community.
> (Proverbs 15:27)

> Don't run up debts. (Romans 13:8)

> The borrower becomes the lender's slave.
> (Proverbs 22:7, NASB)

God also promises to bless us when we use money wisely:

> The king's favor is toward a servant who acts wisely.
> (Proverbs 14:35, NASB)

> Whoever can be trusted with very little can also be trusted with much. (Luke 16:10, NIV)

> A faithful [woman] will be richly blessed.
> (Proverbs 28:20, NIV)

Incredible things happen when we follow a wise money management plan. Our faith increases when we realize our former perception of God is *too small*! God is impossibly generous, unbelievably attentive, and exquisitely sensitive to our needs and wants.

One tiny example from my own life happened when I needed a writing desk. I had sold my first book and was also getting ready to write a novel based on Queen Esther, *Chosen: The Lost Diaries of Queen Esther*. (It's published by NavPress and listed in the Resource Guide.) My papers were scattered all over the house, and I kept losing important information. I had only one spot in the house where I could fit a desk, and I had no cash. My husband's startup business was demanding every last cent we had. I decided that if God can answer big prayers, He could handle the little ones. I asked for a desk to fit in the one corner, and I reminded God that we were broke.

A few weeks later, I noticed that a builder was selling all the furniture in his model homes at a warehouse near me. I got there just as they were closing the sale after a several-day run. The only item left was a beautiful carved Queen Anne desk. It was obviously out of my price range. "How much?" I sighed, knowing I couldn't afford it. The weary staff, anxious to sell the last piece and go home, didn't miss a beat. "Five bucks," they said. And they threw in a lamp and some picture frames! Voila! I asked for a desk, and God sent me a cozy office. I could have bought a desk on credit, but I would have missed a sweet gift from God. That's just one small example of how using money wisely changes the way we see God and grows our faith.

God proved faithful in Esther's story as well, even making her the most wealthy woman in the land. She went into the most important night of her life without a lot of "stuff" to show off, but the king and his court saw *her*, not what she brought. She didn't rely on material goods to bring her love, respect, or attention. We can pass this same legacy on to our daughters as we apply these same lessons to ourselves. God will bless us in comforting, surprising ways.

PREPARING FOR YOUR MEETING

This Month's Beauty Treat: your daughter's choice
*Give her a budget for the evening, including the beauty treat and
restaurant. Let her choose which beauty treat she'd like and where
she'd like to eat, on the condition that she stay within budget. If there's
money left over, she can keep the change.*

At:

Appointment date and time:

Where we'll eat:

Story Stirrers
1. Who taught you about money?

2. What money mistakes have you made? What smart money
moves have you made?

3. How would you like to see your daughter's life be financially
different from or similar to your own?

Go Back for Seconds

1. Both of you carry a small notebook in your purse for one week. Write down every purchase, no matter how small. At the end of the week, compare notes and see how much money you've spent and what for.

2. Develop a budget for yourself.

3. Develop a budget for your daughter: Let her control her school supply money or clothes money.

PREPARE YOUR DAUGHTER FOR THE ESTHER MEETING

1. We'll be getting together for our Esther Year time on this date and time:
2. This month's beauty treat will be: your choice. I'll give you a budget of $____. You pick the beauty treat and restaurant, and if there's money left over at the end of our evening, you keep it.
3. This month's story verse is: Esther 2:15.
4. So when we're together, we're going to be talking about: money.

Love

Real love is an action, a sacrifice of self that honors God.

KEY VERSE:
The king fell in love with Esther far more than with any of his other women or any of the other virgins—he was totally smitten by her.
(Esther 2:17)

Xerxes fell head over heels for Esther, and she became queen. Not a bad ending, right? So why didn't God just add the words "happily ever after" and end the story? Of course, this romance was only an introduction for the great drama yet to come. Romance ushered Esther further down the path of her life's purpose and adventure, but it wasn't the goal or the end point. Esther was being called to love her people and her God.

Today, our daughters are inundated with stories that end with "happily ever after," but we need to tell them the rest of the story. Romance may lead us to true love, but true love is not a feeling; it is an action. Love calls us to sacrifice. When our girls ask how to know whether love is real, we can show them the difference.

Why Did God Give Us Romance, Anyway?
If romance isn't the ultimate goal, why have it at all? I think the first reason God gave us romance is to make the business of life more

enjoyable. As we become adults, we leave our families and marry and spend many years raising babies and trying to live in peace with the opposite sex. God didn't have to build romance into the human DNA. After all, romance is not a necessity in the animal kingdom. In the animal kingdom, it's a short, unromantic drive from meeting to mating. And the end of their story is frequently being served up as dinner, as is the case with the praying mantis. (Except for the male honeybee. If he mates with a female, his privates snap off violently and he dies. Anyone want to bottle that formula for our daughters' dates?)

You, however, are wired to feel good about love, and even to sustain a loving bond during stressful sacrifices. When we fall "in like," our bodies produce norepinephrine and dopamine. These chemicals produce a wonderful, feel-good natural high. That's why in the initial stages of "like," you don't always sleep as much, or eat as much, and you tend to get a little spacey. It's a wonderful feeling, and it sure helps cushion all those blows to our pride and hearts as we face rejection and disappointments.

When we move from romance to real love, the relationship becomes more routine, and our bodies begin to produce oxytocin instead. The edge of the romance wears off, but your body helps facilitate the continued relationship by secreting the hormone that helps bonding. Oxytocin is also the same hormone produced at birth and during nursing to help moms bond with their babies. Think about that for a moment: A mother with a newborn is a great demonstration of selfless love. She's not eating, showering, or sleeping, but she's giving 100 percent to caring for her newborn. The baby can't do anything in return but make more work. And through it all, the mom's body is helping to soothe her roughened nerves by secreting a hormone that helps her to love.

Romance? That was just a precursor to this moment of sacrifice. Remember, researchers have documented that during stressful times, women react by wanting to nurture and love someone else. It's called the "tend and befriend" response and is believed to be rooted in our unique body chemistry.[1] We're designed to be ready for the sacrifices of real love.

The body is created to produce chemicals that make romance a delight and help take the edge off the difficult business of loving others, especially when it comes to self-sacrifice. How gracious of God to supply us with so many wonderful-feeling hormones for the process of loving another!

Going All the Way

I love the following description of true love from Dr. Craig Glickman's incredible book *Solomon's Song of Love*. When a high school boy has just confessed he "went all the way" and had sex with his girlfriend, a wise adult tells him:

> That's not going all the way at all. . . . I'll tell you what going all the way is. There's a guy in my neighborhood who has five kids, and his wife is now in a wheelchair. He gets the kids off to school each morning, sells insurance all day to make a living, then comes home and makes dinner for the family. And at the end of the evening, he looks his wife in the eye and tells her he loves her. I know he means it, too, because he tells me he's the luckiest guy he knows to have been blessed with her. *That's* what going all the way is.[2]

This is the defining moment where romance and real love part ways. Romance is a feeling, and it's fleeting. Real love is an action, a sacrifice of self that honors God. How did Esther and her story illustrate this principle?

- Esther sacrificed in love by living in the harem and submitting to Hegai's instruction.

- Mordecai sacrificed in love by spending his days trying to get updates on Esther's condition inside—he never abdicated his responsibility for her.
- Mordecai sacrificed in love by refusing to honor an evil man despite what his culture was doing.
- Mordecai sacrificed in love by reporting a threat on the king's life, even though this was the king who had taken Esther from her home.
- Esther sacrificed in love by risking her life to confront the king and the evil Haman.
- Esther sacrificed in love by fasting and praying for three days before the confrontation so that she could seek God first.
- Esther sacrificed in love by confronting the king with respect and humility so that he would not be embarrassed for sentencing her people to die.

In the story of Esther, we see over and over that she and Mordecai were called on to forget themselves and their own agendas and instead serve others. What we may call romance in the story—being sought out for your beauty and marrying a wealthy king—fades in comparison to the rich legacy Esther has left us now. God doesn't condemn romance; He simply doesn't stop there. Romance may lead to real love, but real love is about what we do, not what we feel.

Purity and Grace

When most moms talk about romance and love, the subject of purity is never far behind. Shannon Ethridge, author of *Preparing Your Daughter for Every Woman's Battle* and a sexual integrity advocate, says moms should focus on giving their daughters lots of accurate information. Shannon says,

Moms may hesitate, saying they don't want to awaken sexual desires in their daughters. But there's a big difference between ignorance and innocence. Innocence is a state of the heart, and no amount of healthy, good information can change that. Ignorance is a state of mind, and keeping a girl ignorant robs her of the tools she'll need to maintain her innocence.

Moms can help their daughters hold on to their innocence by breaking through the wall of silence we keep around our sexuality. Shannon says,

> It's important for moms to tell their girls that temptation is normal. You can be one hundred percent committed to sexual purity and still be tempted. There's nothing wrong with you if you're tempted.

Breaking through this silence will also allow your girl to reach her generation in a powerful way.

How Purity Saves Others

Like Esther, your daughter is part of a larger story, and her actions will impact many.

Statistics tell us some of your daughter's friends are already sexually active. Here's what they are experiencing:

- Sexually active teens are less likely to be happy, more likely to be depressed, more likely to commit suicide. [3]
- Every day 8,000 teens will get infected with a new STD.[4]
- 34 percent of teen girls will get pregnant at least once before age twenty.[5]

Some girls don't understand that they don't have to earn love or compete for attention, so they are vulnerable to bad choices and the consequences that follow. They hurt themselves and don't think anyone will grieve with them—they're afraid of facing condemnation, so they suffer in silence. You can reach the next generation by talking with your daughter and encouraging her to reach out to others. Helping your daughter to understand the generous dose of love and grace that is always available despite our mistakes will prepare her to be an Esther in her own generation, rescuing one broken heart at a time.

The Temptation of Purity

There is a temptation in the church to make purity a bargaining chip. A virgin bride is "worth more," and a bride who has had sex is "worth less." This equation isn't about purity as the Bible defines it, which is a state of heart and mind. Virginity until marriage is an *expression* of purity, but purity and virginity are not the same thing. Because we've made purity and virginity interchangeable terms, we've effectively said to girls that if they make a mistake, they are no longer pure and there is no longer any value in trying to be pure. They might as well live it up since they've ruined themselves, right?

I was on a coveted date with a very handsome minister once. He was delighted with a lesson he had taught his students: He passed around a plate of cookies and had each student pick one and take a bite. Then they placed the bitten cookie back on the plate. After all the students had bitten a piece off of a cookie, he passed the plate around again to see who wanted the cookies now. "No one did!" my clueless minister exclaimed, beaming at me in the moonlight. "I told them that's what happened when they had sex—they were no longer wanted by anyone else!" I immediately had what my family fondly calls a "face cramp" and told him in thinly veiled terms he was crazy. He never asked me out again. (Which is just as well—how would I have ever told him my own cookie had a few nibbles around the edges?)

The handsome minister had missed the whole point of the gospel: that we are not judged by what we've done, but by what Jesus did for us. We're forgiven and made into entirely new creations when we accept Jesus as our God and Savior. Grace needs to be emphasized when we're discussing purity with our daughters. It's a dangerous situation when the world preaches wild unrestraint and the church damns sin with no talk of grace or redemption. I don't think you have to share explicit details from your own life that you are uncomfortable with and that would make your daugther weird out on you. Parenting expert Mary DeMuth tells us, "Pray about the timing and manner in which you tell your daughter certain life stories. Sometimes she's too young to hear your story. Sometimes she needs just a snapshot, other times a full-length movie." But let's never discuss purity without mentioning grace, too.

If your daughter understands grace, she will be able to share the true message of purity and the cleansing power of God's redemption. Teens can't escape a destructive lifestyle until they know where to run. By teaching grace as vigorously as we teach purity and by breaking through the wall of silence that forces girls to struggle alone, we equip our daughters to lead a brokenhearted friend into the safe haven of God's redemption.

The Gift of Purity

Shannon makes one last point for our daughters: "The gift of purity is overwhelming confidence. Girls who live out purity are confident to approach God, relationships, and their dreams." This is how God wants us to live and approach Him: "Let's walk right up to him and get what he is so ready to give. Take the mercy, accept the help" (Hebrews 4:16). God designed us to be confident, and purity helps us live that out.

What girl doesn't want to be more confident? Girls search for confidence by changing their looks, their weight, their friends . . .

Could it be that purity has held the key for them all along? Girls may confuse purity as something they are committed to in order to please their parents or their future husband, but God is determined to bless them right now, as they remain committed to the battle for integrity. He will give them the desires of their hearts.

Teaching our daughters to understand the gift of romance in light of the sacrifice of real love encourages them to search for the story beyond happily ever after. If they are going to be Esthers in their own generation, they have to first understand that real love is sacrifice.

PREPARING FOR YOUR MEETING

This Month's Beauty Treat: finding the perfect perfume
There are so many options, but your daughter will probably find one that's just right for her. What connections can you make between romance and perfume? How wonderful to find and fall in love with just the right scent? How fleeting can it be? How some perfumes stink—and sometimes you just have to take a break from it all? Be as silly and playful as you feel and save the serious conversation for dessert.

At:

Appointment date and time:

Where we'll eat:

Story Stirrers

1. When you were younger, which did you think was more important: romance or love? What do you think now, and who or what changed your mind?

2. When have you experienced sacrificial love? When have you experienced romance? Which had more of an impact on your life?

3. What does it mean to you that the gospel is centered around the sacrificial love of a Savior?

Go Back for Seconds

1. What can you do with your daughter to show her the effects of romance without sacrificial love? Can you volunteer at a crisis pregnancy center?

2. Look up the website of the Oriental Museum of Chicago: http://oi.uchicago.edu/OI/MUS/PA/IRAN/PAAI/IMAGES/PER/HX/PAAI_Harem_Xerxes_1.html. You'll see pictures of Xerxes' harem. (Xerxes being the probable king from the story of Esther, although no archaeological evidence to attest to this

story has been found in the ruins.) Harems may seem a thing of the ancient past, but modern sex-slave rings still exist today. You can learn more and donate to help set a girl free from exploitation at: www.ijm.org, the home page for International Justice Mission. For information on protecting American girls from the exploitation of pornography, visit the National Coalition for the Protection of Children and Families at www.nationalcoalition. org. A donation to either organization is an incredible gift to the world.

Prepare Your Daughter for the Esther Meeting

1. We'll be getting together for our Esther Year time on this date and time:
2. This month's beauty treat will be: the perfect perfume.
3. This month's story verse is: Esther 2:17.
4. So when we're together, we're going to be talking about: love versus romance.

Courage

Courage calls us to trust God in the midst of fear.

KEY VERSES:

Mordecai sent her this message: "Don't think that just because you live in the king's house you're the one Jew who will get out of this alive. If you persist in staying silent at a time like this, help and deliverance will arrive for the Jews from someplace else." (Esther 4:13-14)

Poor Esther. She's been through a lot already in our story, and now she's facing the biggest crisis yet. Understandably, she doesn't want to risk death by intervening with the king's plans. She probably felt a great deal of fear, and when she begged Mordecai to think of another plan, he rebuked her. "You can't run away from this," he said, but we can guess that Esther probably wanted nothing more than to run. Mordecai didn't tell Esther not to be afraid; he was making an impassioned plea for Esther to act wisely.

Fear is a strange emotion, unlike anything else we feel. Most other emotions are meant to be shared. Negative ones dissipate when shared with a friend. Happy ones are sustained. But fear doesn't want anyone coming to the party. It wants us alone. It wants to terrorize us. It wants to quickly force us to run away or make a rash decision, but courage calls us to move beyond our fear and act wisely.

Why We Can't "Share" Fear Away

Unlike fear, most forms of suffering are relieved when we share our burden:

> When Anne Morrow Lindbergh's infant son was kidnapped and murdered, only the story of the mustard seed helped her. A woman who has lost her baby asks a holy man if there is a cure for her grief. "Yes," he replies. "You must find a house that has never known sorrow, take a mustard seed from that house, and then you will be cured." The woman spent the rest of her life looking, but could never find a house that had not known sorrow.[1]

Suffering is meant to be shared; when we feel the bond of humanity, our pain is eased. But we can't share fear away. I can tell you my fears, but they won't go away, and yours won't be lessened, either. Fear wants to keep us frozen. It wants to control us. It usually wants us to run from what we're being asked to do. That's why courage begins with a deep breath and a willingness to quietly listen to wisdom.

Mordecai must have understood this. He warned Esther that fear would hiss at her to run. Fear would push her in the opposite direction from Mordecai's plan of action. Esther had to master her fear if she were going to save the nation. She had to find courage to do the right thing.

What are your fears, and what are they telling you to do? Does God sound like the voice of Mordecai in your ear, urging you to take courage, pause, and choose wisely? What are our basic fears, and what actions can we take to be free of them?

Fear of Confrontation

I hate confrontation. Fear tells me to avoid it. It warns me of the dangers of speaking up:

- I don't want someone to think less of me.
- I don't want to draw attention to myself.
- I'm afraid of being harmed physically or emotionally.

Fear yells at me to run away, but courage calls me to act. The voice of God tells me to walk toward Him—and He often leads me right through the middle of the minefield.

Some days the minefield is in my mind and heart as I wrestle with my right or responsibility to say "no." It's not a word that always comes easily to me, and I know it doesn't come easily for many other women as well. Author Gavin de Becker encourages us as moms to reclaim this word for ourselves and our daughters:

Of all the lessons a mother might pass to her daughter, the most valuable can be summed up with just two letters: N-O. Though the word No is one of the most potent in our language, it is among the least popular. In part, that's because most of us grew up associating that word with not getting what we wanted. Most kids hate the word, but as they grow, there is exceptional value from learning to love it. Though perhaps hard to imagine, this single word can play a central role in safety, particularly for young women, and particularly when she comes to dating age. We have to teach young women that "No" is a complete sentence. This is not as simple as it may appear. Understand that when a man in our culture says No, it's usually the end of a discussion, but when a woman says No, it's the beginning of a negotiation. If the culture taught (and then allowed) teenage girls to explicitly reject and to explicitly say no, or if more of them took that power early in every relationship, stalking and date-rape cases would decline dramatically.[2]

It's strange, isn't it, that when our girls were babies, they spent most of their days saying "no"? Saying "no" gave them a sense of security and power, believing they could reject anything they didn't want (like baths and vegetables). Mr. de Becker was right: We hated being told "no." But we sure loved saying it!

When did we lose "no"? Was it elementary school when cliques formed and we feared being alone? Was it high school when we feared losing a boyfriend or being uncool? Maybe those are stories you'll share later. Reclaiming "no" is a powerful rite of passage for moms and a powerful legacy to pass along to your daughter.

Fear of Failure and Rejection

I inherited my response to failure from my dad. He's a mad, mad scientist. He loves failure. It electrifies him—sometimes quite literally. He's never happier than when he's failed at something, because he loves a good chase. His face lights up, he mumbles to himself, and he dashes through the house for quick lunch breaks—all because he senses there's a battle to be waged, an elusive victory on the horizon. He loves tackling the obstacles and finally discovering the hidden nugget of knowledge he was missing. Following his example, fear of failure is not as much of a problem for me. I still feel it, but I am more compelled to enjoy the thrill of the chase.

But the failure of rejection—ouch! It took me years to understand God's purpose in rejection. Rejection is one of God's most powerful tools in shaping us for our destiny. Esther was not immune from it. Her story begins by one woman being rejected, and Esther quickly gets a taste of it herself. When Mordecai calls her to confront the king, she tells him it's been thirty days since she was called to him. Xerxes had many women in his harems. No one could see him when they wished—they had to wait for him to call. If he never called, they never saw him again. For some reason, Xerxes didn't call her for a month. Perhaps he was busy, offended, or interested in another woman, but Esther felt the sting of rejection. It caused her to hesitate when the time for courage came.

Most people who have accomplished great things in life have experienced a great deal of rejection along the way. As a mom, this is a painful truth. I want to shield my daughters from rejection, and they certainly don't want to face it. But if God answers my prayer and never allows rejection to teach my daughters, I may be trading away their destiny. They simply cannot become all they are meant to be without enduring rejection. So I want to give them hope. I want to encourage them that rejection is not a sign they are unloved, but that God is doing something greater in them. I want to teach them to endure rejection because it is a sign that God is moving in their lives. Every closed door forces us all further down the path, getting us closer to the great calling on our lives. When we're rejected, we have to turn away from people and things to fulfill us and rely once more on God. God gets our full attention, and in that moment we're teachable. He can reveal a new, unexplored path to us. Rejection can awaken you, and your girl, to who you were created to be.

Fear of Abandonment

I sat in a counselor's office. I had been having panic attacks and wanted to understand why. The counselor made a long list for me of my fears and the consequence each one led to: If I didn't perform, I might be abandoned. If I didn't look right, I might be abandoned. If I didn't attend the right functions, I might be abandoned. Finally she looked at me and said, "What's so terrible about being alone?" I squirmed in the chair and looked out the window. I couldn't think of an answer. Wouldn't it mean a chance to catch up on laundry? If so, sign me up!

The reason I couldn't think of an answer that day is that this fear makes no spiritual sense. Being abandoned hurts and we all want to avoid pain, but the reality is, we're never truly alone. God lives within us, is around us, and works through us. Fear of abandonment probably started in the garden. Since Satan was in the garden, perhaps he saw Adam and Eve being formed and witnessed God's proclamation that it wasn't good for us to be alone. Satan's been threatening us with that ever since. But it's not going to happen. We may have left the garden, but God has promised never to leave us: God assured us, "I'll never let you down, never walk off and leave you" (Hebrews 13:5). We are never alone. God will never abandon us and he is faithful to supply all our needs.

Fears Can Be Inherited

Fears are often learned responses, and we inherit them just like we inherit the good china, photo albums, and quirky behaviors. It reminds me of a friend who always cut the ends off a ham before she stuck the ham in the oven. It made no sense. It wasted food. Finally, she asked her mother about this weird habit she had inherited. Long ago, the mother said, grandmom's oven wasn't big enough for a whole ham so she cut the ends off the ham to get it to fit. And the girls in the family had been doing it ever since.

What fears have you inherited? (I'd love to tell you mine, but my mom would kill me! Some conversations are just between moms and daughters, right?) The good news is that when one woman in the family takes on that fear and demolishes it, the other women are more likely to do the same thing. My grandmother is exceptionally smart and wanted to go to college and be a scientist, but she was told women couldn't do that. Her advisors were fearful about her future. My mom wanted to go to college for years but didn't. I was the first generation to go to college, and as soon as I was about to graduate, my mom enrolled herself. She also got better grades than I did, but then, she wasn't hanging out at fraternity parties till 2 a.m. (Of course, if she reads this, I didn't either, Mom. I was *studying* until 2 a.m.)

Courage compels us to take action, and we may set more than

ourselves free. Esther's story shows us that one brave action can save a nation.

God's Plan for Fear

God does mention several things we are never to fear, and one thing we are:

1. Do not fear any situation, event, calamity, or evil (see Psalm 23:4).
2. Do not fear any person (see Psalm 27:1).
3. But do fear Me (see 2 Kings 17:36).

If we are commanded to fear the Lord, what does that mean? I don't want to be afraid of Him. Isn't that a complete contradiction of a loving Shepherd who rescues the one lost sheep?

Fear is an acknowledgment that something—or someone—has power over us. We're not afraid of a teacup poodle, but we're afraid of a pit bull. The difference is how we've assessed their power over us. A pit bull can hurt us. A teacup poodle is just cute. God tells us not to be afraid of people because fear of people is rooted in the false belief that they have power over us. We're told not to fear circumstances or evil because they don't have power over us, either. Only God does. Reserving our fear for Him alone doesn't mean we're afraid to approach Him—it means we acknowledge that no one and no thing has power over us except Him. Reserving our fear for God alone is an act of worship.

Preparing for Your Meeting

This Month's Beauty Treat: jewelry shopping

Choose a few tasteful pieces for school, work, and evenings out. It's better to choose pieces that are not made with real gems, because very soon we're going to pass along a more valuable piece from our own jewelry box. Now is the time to choose pieces that won't be terribly missed if they go missing.

In Esther's day, women wore special jewelry to protect them from their fears: the spirits they imagined or diseases that might strike their family. Thank God that you have a gift even Esther herself lacked: a deeper revelation of the source of those fears (Satan) and the Source of all courage (Jesus). Our daughters are free today, freer than Esther, not merely because of political changes, but because of God's redeeming plan in Jesus.

At:

Appointment date and time:

Where we'll eat:

Story Stirrers

1. What fears have you overcome? How did you do it?

2. Are there fears that are part of your family's legacy? How have these shaped behaviors and relationships? What are you doing to break free of them?

3. How have you seen God at work in the midst of your fears? What have you learned about His character?

Go Back for Seconds

1. Tackle a fear with your daughter. If you're both afraid of public speaking, agree to give speeches at a retreat. If you're both afraid of heights, sign up for a rock-climbing class together.

2. Sign up with your daughter for a weekend self-defense workshop.

3. Both of you write down every fear you have, and then burn the list in your backyard or fireplace. Celebrate that your fears are nothing more than smoke and ashes and can't control you any longer.

PREPARE YOUR DAUGHTER
FOR THE ESTHER MEETING

1. We'll be getting together for our Esther Year time on this date and time:

2. This month's beauty treat will be: costume jewelry—but on another night not far from now, you'll receive a very different type of jewelry!

3. This month's story verses are: Esther 4:13-14.

4. So when we're together, we're going to be talking about: courage.

Purpose

If we are faithful, God will reveal His plan in His perfect timing.

KEY VERSE:
Who knows? Maybe you were made queen for just such a time as this.
(Esther 4:14)

In *The Purpose-Driven Life*, Rick Warren explains our search for purpose:

> We typically begin at the wrong starting point—ourselves.
> We ask self-centered questions like What do *I* want to be?
> What should *I* do with *my* life? What are *my* goals, *my* ambi-
> tions, *my* dreams for *my* future? But focusing on ourselves
> will never reveal our life's purpose. . . . Contrary to what
> many popular books, movies, and seminars tell you, you won't
> discover your life's meaning by looking within yourself.[1]

Recently I did a survey with moms to discover what they felt and thought about their destiny and purpose. There was an uncertain, fearful undercurrent in some of their answers. Destiny, life purpose. Aren't those terms for titans of industry, celebrities, or the unusually gifted? Moms were hesitant to use that term for their own lives. Somehow, they felt having a destiny, or a grand purpose, just wasn't quite relevant to their lives. They couldn't look at any one accomplishment and say, "That was my destiny."

I understand completely. Even the accomplishments I'm most proud of fall short of what I would call "destiny" or my life's "purpose." I'm left with a feeling that there is something more, something lacking in my accomplishments. The hint of what's missing is found in the first chapter of Ephesians:

> He set it all out before us in Christ, a long-range plan in
> which everything would be brought together and
> summed up in him, everything in deepest heaven,
> everything on planet earth. It's in Christ that we find
> out who we are and what we are living for.
>
> (EPHESIANS 1:9-11)

Our purpose is part of a long-range plan involving the deepest realms and dimensions of the spiritual and physical worlds. The *New International Version* refers to this as the "mystery" of God's will. We need to teach our daughters that a great deal of their purpose will not be revealed in this lifetime. It's wrapped up in a long-range plan, a mystery of how God is using them to impact realms they may not even know exist.

But we're *taught* that purpose is tangible—that at the end of our lives, we should be able to point to a building, a body of work, or a medical breakthrough and say, "That was mine." Christians sometimes do each other a disservice by proclaiming that "God has a plan for your life." He does. But that doesn't mean we can understand it. God's will for us is different from His purpose. He wills that we submit and trust so that He can use us in ways we don't know about and can't understand yet. The Christian life is one of daring, daily leaps into the unknown.

The blessing we can communicate to our daughters here is that they can relax about finding the "one" purpose or plan God has set out for them. God has promised to use them. God has promised to guide them in their daily walk (see Proverbs 4:10-12). But God hasn't promised to reveal all His mysteries right now.

Mordecai's most famous utterance, "Who knows? Maybe you were made queen for just such a time as this?" hints at just this mystery and the incredible possibilities lurking all around us. Esther could not have humanly understood how God orchestrated all the events of her life to bring her to that moment. Could she have understood how He arranged her DNA to create an appearance especially pleasing to this one king? Could she have understood how her people were exiled and came to live in that exact place at that exact time? Could she have understood how each family in the kingdom would be changed when she procured their salvation? Could she have understood how her story would change each woman who heard it in the future? The story was simply too large for her because she was human. Our story dwarfs us as well. It is so grand and large that the best we can hope for on a clear day is a glimpse of its shadow.

Profession Versus Purpose

Another clue the Bible gives us about purpose is found in Matthew 22:37-40 when Jesus sums up the Scriptures into two famous commands: Love God and love your neighbor. This is your life's most important, fundamental purpose:

1. You were put here to love God.
2. You were put here to love others.

Everything will flow from these two directives. The question may not be, "*What* do I *do?*" but "*How* can I love?" God may have called you to be a doctor, a writer, a mother, a nursery volunteer, or a sales clerk. That's what you do. But your purpose is different. Your purpose is love. Esther loved. She loved a king by submitting to him although he might not accept her nationality. She loved Mordecai by submitting to his authority. She loved her people by trying to save them. And this love was going to ask something else of her.

The Sacrifice of Purpose

What have we already learned about love during this Esther Year? We've already learned that love requires a sacrifice. Since your purpose is love, sacrifice won't be far behind. God will ask us to sacrifice as part of His purpose for our lives. Some sacrifices are voluntary, others are blows dealt to us by life, and still others are sacrifices in spirit—a willingness to give something, or someone, away. Consider all the sacrifices Esther had to make before her purpose in Xerxes' palace was revealed:

1. Esther sacrificed a normal family. She had to submit to an uncle who raised her because she had been orphaned.
2. Esther sacrificed a normal adolescence to live in Xerxes' harem.
3. Esther sacrificed a chance for marriage when she went to the harem—if Xerxes rejected her, she could never be free to marry someone else.
4. Esther was willing to sacrifice her life to interrupt Xerxes and beg for his help.

Esther is one of the most celebrated women in history, but she made great sacrifices. If she had fought against any one of those circumstances, she probably would have lost her place in God's purpose. Love leads us to sacrifice, and sacrifice leads us to our destiny.

Patient and Present

Esther's life was marked by confusing interruptions, heartache, and endless—and seemingly meaningless—preparation for one night with a man she'd never met. Her world defined her purpose early and completely. God had other plans. He gave her a new identity, changing her from just another woman who would disappear into the ages into a woman every generation would celebrate for thousands of years. She was faithful and *patient*, and God was faithful and *present*.

Our girls face intense pressure to pick a career, a focus, a future, a major. But discovering all of these capacities can take patience. Exploring options takes patience, and so does building skill sets. We even have to learn what we need to learn! When I first wanted to be a writer, I gave myself a year to learn how books are published before I even began the process of actually writing one.

For our girls, the pressure to pick can undermine the patience they need for exploration. They may see some goals as unattainable simply because there isn't enough time to investigate them well. It's a good thing to give our daughters permission to "try without buying." When a girl closes off her options too soon, she may make poor choices:

> Many teenage pregnancies aren't accidental but intentional because of girls who see no life goals other than being a mother as realistically within their reach.[2]

God gives us the freedom to experiment with our interests and profession because He guarantees that His purpose will come to pass no matter what we do (see Proverbs 19:21; Isaiah 46:10). God is actively blessing us right now. He's not standing on the sidelines waiting to see how we play the game, ready to punish us if we make mistakes. If we're on His team, He's going to coach us. Whatever skills or materials we need to accomplish His plan, He'll provide. When we love and walk with Him, we can release any fear of missing His plan for us.

Our girls need patience as they try to understand God's purpose for their own lives. One lesson I learned early in my mother's kitchen is that the bigger the recipe, the longer it cooks. You can't feed a crowd unless you give yourself plenty of time to prepare and plenty of time for the oven. In life, if you want to go big, you've got to slow down. Finally, we can assure our daughters that the mystery of God's bigger purpose will always leave a bit of wonder and questioning in our hearts. That's not a sign we've missed Him. It's a sign that He's not finished with us yet. There are still blessings and adventures ahead.

PREPARING FOR YOUR MEETING

This Month's Beauty Treat: wardrobe/fashion consultation
A major department store will probably have someone on staff to help. Moms, we know that showing too much skin is often related to having too little confidence in who you are and why you're here. Girls who feel they have fewer choices in life often make poorer ones. When a girl understands what looks best with her frame and coloring, she can present her best self to the world.

At:

Appointment date and time:

Where we'll eat:

Story Stirrers

1. How would you define your purpose? How has this definition changed since you were a teen?

2. When in your life have you felt off course and directionless? What was that like for you? How did you get back on track?

3. As you think about your teen years, what were the noticeable differences between girls who were pursuing their interests and girls who weren't?

Go Back for Seconds

1. Author Tim Elmore speaks frequently of arranging "career and mentor" days for his daughter. He arranged for his daughter to spend a day with different godly women in different professions. This is a great way for her to explore different options and see what ultimately might interest her.

2. Create a personal mission statement. What do you both feel God has equipped you with to love others? How do you want to live out your purpose with your gifts?

PREPARE YOUR DAUGHTER
FOR THE ESTHER MEETING

1. We'll be getting together for our Esther Year time on this date and time:
2. This month's beauty treat will be: wardrobe consultation.
3. This month's story verse is: Esther 4:14.
4. So when we're together, we're going to be talking about: purpose.

Faith

Faith calls us to believe that what God says is true.

KEY VERSE:
If I die, I die. (Esther 4:16)

When Esther decided to approach the king about his unwise decision, she risked not only rejection, but death. And it was probably death by impalement. Esther had not been called into the king's presence in about a month. He had a huge harem and was likely sleeping with other women, many of whom were desperate to steal Esther's crown. After all, Xerxes had already banished his first queen. He could do it again.

If Esther approached the king without being summoned, the king could sentence her to death immediately or extend his scepter and allow her to live. Approaching the king was a rash act for a queen who knew this man's history. He did not react well to women who embarrassed him. If he didn't like being disturbed by her, for any reason, Esther's story would have an abrupt, unpleasant ending.

Mordecai's earlier response indicates that Esther would have preferred to avoid confrontation and run from the problem. She certainly didn't like Mordecai's plan of disturbing the king. She didn't have the kind of faith that made her "yes" an immediate response, and I'm thankful for that. She had to work up the willingness, just like most of us. Willingness heralds the first little steps of faith.

What Faith Is

- Faith is a gift from God:

> For it is by grace you have been saved, through faith—and
> this not from yourselves, it is the gift of God.
>
> (EPHESIANS 2:8, NIV)

Because God does not give to us as the world gives (see John 14:27), we may not understand this gift. How do we use our faith? Do we feel it first and then act, or act first and feel it later? I think it all comes down to a simple (but not easy) first step: belief.

- Faith is believing God's Word.

Faith is believing that God's Word is true and His promises will come to pass in our lives. Every morning I read the Bible while I exercise on my ski machine. (Yes, it takes coordination to do that all at once!) As I make my prayer requests and name them off one by one, I am constantly challenged as I stare at the Bible open in front of me. "If I really believed everything it says was true," I ask myself, "would I be praying about this?" If I believed God when He said He would provide for me, would I be praying about my financial fears? If I really believed I was totally accepted and beloved by God, would I be praying about feeling insecure? Over and over my greatest struggle each morning isn't getting another tough workout finished, but struggling to let go of doubt and absolutely believe. Belief is tough work, because all day long little doubts will creep in, and I have to constantly remind myself, "I believe."

Faith is not a feeling. Faith is not self-confidence. It's not a belief in ourselves, but a belief that God is within, and around, and for us. We may never feel confident when we step out in faith. Esther's story doesn't give us a picture of a woman who is brimming with self-confidence and pleased to present herself unannounced. Like love, faith is a decision before it is an action. We choose to believe God's Word, and then we act on our belief. Esther chose to believe God would triumph even if she died, and so she was willing to face death.

Faith is also a response to the desires God has given us:

> Delight yourself in the LORD and he will give you the
> desires of your heart.
>
> (PSALM 37:4, NIV)

To delight in God means He holds us spellbound. He lures us out of ourselves. Sometimes this means God will give us desires that are far out of our reach and abilities. There's simply no human possibility of achieving these goals and dreams, and yet God places them in our hearts and gives us a burning desire to see them come to pass. We have to rely on faith to step out in willingness. We have to rely on faith as we step into the unknown, believing that God will meet us there and part the sea of resistance and conflict. Esther would have understood this dilemma well: She wanted to save her people, but she could not control the king's reaction if she broke protocol. To step into the king's presence and risk a brutal death required a willingness to receive the gift of faith and the willingness to take that first step into the unknown.

Faith Is God's Strength

Esther began by emptying herself of her own strength. Her fast weakened her and forced her to depend on God's strength and provision. The ancient historian Josephus tells us that Esther was so weak from her fast that her handmaidens had to follow behind her to carry her robes.

I've done a lot of dumb things in my own strength. In fact, every dumb thing I've ever done was in my own strength! But the times when I have relied completely on God's strength, I've experienced miracles. Some miracles were as minor as keeping my mouth shut, and some were much more profound. It's maddening for me to be powerless and depleted of all strength, but I wouldn't trade the answers to prayer I've received in those moments for all the riches in the world.

One example that will always stay in my mind happened when my friends and I were caring for our beloved friend Beth. Beth had breast cancer and was not expected to live. Everything had been done to save her. It was agonizing to hear of every new avenue of healing pursued and the continual bad news. We took meals to her and her family, and we organized giant prayer-and-fasting days. And yet the news from the doctors was never what we wanted. Finally, one week a much smaller group of us decided to pray and fast. I felt weary and discouraged. But there was something different about this fast. We didn't ask everyone to join us. We sensed that we had all done everything we could. All we had left was God's strength. We could do absolutely nothing in our own power as we begged God to "show up" and intervene. I took a meal to Beth soon after, and tears welled in my eyes as she told me what had happened during our fast. She was in terrible pain and the medications made it hard for her to stay awake and to interact with her children. She faced a continual battle: Either be in terrible pain and see her children, or experience relief but lose those last fleeting hours.

From the time we started the fast until the time we ended it, the pain miraculously left Beth's body. She was able to play with her children and enjoy a wonderful day with them. I still weep when I think of the power of relying on nothing but God and how God blessed us all. Beth died shortly after. We didn't understand her death. We didn't want it. Faith didn't keep the reality of death away. Faith gave us the courage to live in spite of the realities of death. Faith extended an invitation to God to show His strength because ours was gone. How many more miracles have I missed because I forgot to empty myself of my own strength and rely on God's instead? How much more could He do in me, through me, and around me?

Esther found a way to empty herself of her own strength and seek God's instead for her step of faith. How is God calling you and me to do the same? How can you help your daughter let go of her own strength and cling to God's instead? Let's begin to think of how we can encourage her to abandon the worldly pursuit of strength and focus on the pursuit of faith instead.

Worldly strength produces short-term, interesting results (at its best). People receive praise and recognition from their peers. But faith produces astonishing displays of power that have eternal impact. God receives praise and recognition.

Carol Kent understands the power of faith, especially faith during a crisis, and she writes about her experience in *When I Lay My Isaac Down: Unshakable Faith in Unthinkable Circumstances.* (See the Resource Guide for more information.)

My son was arrested for a heinous crime and it was the faith I had BEFORE the crisis that sustained me through his trial and through his eventual conviction for first degree murder. It was Scripture I memorized long before my trial that constantly reminded me of the faith in God I knew was the Truth.

Carol encourages us to practice God's encouragement to walk with the wise (see Proverbs 13:20):

Observing people who hold tightly to their faith builds our own 'faith-muscle.' Choosing faith in a dark hour gives unexpected empowerment—because we know we are going to win in the long run. The enemy fails to defeat us or close our mouths, so when we act in faith, even when we question why God allowed something bad to happen, our spiritual strength brings a joyful surprise—to us and those who observe us.

Our girls may experience little tastes of Esther's dilemma every day. They can face a thousand fearful risks and rejections at school: auditions, teasing, grading, judgments. Getting out of bed can be an act of faith some days! We can teach them Esther's secret of faith: it's not what we feel. It's not always our first reaction. Faith is the willingness to believe, and when we believe our stories take a wonderful turn.

PREPARING FOR YOUR MEETING

This Month's Beauty Treat: pedicure

Let's pamper those hard-working feet! If we're going to get anywhere, it's our feet that will do the work. Faith is the same way: It takes hard work and is often unseen, but it's impossible to move forward without it.

At:

Appointment date and time:

Where we'll eat:

Story Stirrers

1. What difficult decision have you made that required you to rely on faith?

2. What actions have you taken that required nothing but God's strength?

3. Have you ever had regrets from acting by faith or relying on God's strength?

4. Have you ever had regrets from relying on your own strength and ability?

Go Back for Seconds

1. Together with your daughter, make a list of the top ten things you'd like to see done in your own life, in the life of your family, and in the world. Set one day aside to pray specifically over these lists and ask God how you can act in faith and in His strength to achieve any of these goals.

2. Have you ever fasted? Fasting involves giving up food (or another source of strength and comfort) for a set period of time in order to devote yourself more fully to prayer and seeking God's comfort and strength. A recommended guide to fasting is included in the Resource Guide. Try fasting for a meal, or a day, and ask for a fresh outpouring of God's strength in place of your own.

PREPARE YOUR DAUGHTER
FOR THE ESTHER MEETING

1. We'll be getting together for our Esther Year time on this date and time:
2. This month's beauty treat will be: pedicure.
3. This month's story verse is: Esther 4:16.
4. So when we're together, we're going to be talking about: faith.

Wisdom

Wisdom is worth any price and brings lasting peace.

KEY VERSES:
The king asked, "And what's your desire, Queen Esther? What do you
want? Ask and it's yours—even if it's half my kingdom!"

"If it please the king," said Esther, "let the king come with Haman to a
dinner I've prepared for him."(Esther 5:3-4)

A nation hung in the balance. In the streets outside the palace, notices
had been posted in every public place that a date had been set for the
execution of the Jews. Mothers wept as they tucked their children in
at night. Fathers despaired, knowing they had no way to protect their
families. There was no place they could run for refuge—the Persian
empire stretched thousands of miles in every direction. And every
day was bringing every family closer to the edge of a sword.

Esther understood the savagery of the situation and how desperate her people were, but she didn't act immediately. She began by fasting for three full days before even speaking to her husband the king.
She wanted to have this ordeal over with. She could have confronted
Haman and the king on the first night, and she knew everyone
outside the banquet hall was waiting to know the outcome. An entire
nation of Jews would be slaughtered if she wasn't successful, and
there wasn't much time to save them. "Urgency" was the theme for

the evening, and yet, a small voice told her to wait. It didn't seem to offer any explanation. It probably didn't offer any promises. The time just wasn't right. What courage Esther had to listen! No matter how high the stakes, no matter how much pressure is on you to choose, you must listen for the quiet voice of wisdom.

How do you recognize true wisdom that is from God? God gives us a checklist in James 3:14-17 (NIV):
The wisdom that comes from *heaven* is:

- Pure
- Peace-loving
- Considerate
- Submissive
- Full of mercy
- Full of good fruit
- Impartial
- Sincere

Earthly wisdom is rooted in:

- Bitter envy
- Selfish ambition

How Do You Get This Wisdom from Heaven?

The first step is to admit what is in your heart. James 3:14 tells us that if we are holding on to selfish ambition or envy, we should admit it openly. Confession drains the fuel that runs our secrets. You can be emptied only if you first confess what is in your heart. Next, ask:

If any of you lacks wisdom, he should ask God, who gives
generously to all without finding fault, and it will be
given to him.

(JAMES 1:5, NIV)

God promises to be generous in answering your prayer. He promises not to fault you for asking. It's not your job to magically know
what to do. It's your job to ask and then patiently listen.

When "What If?" Lingers
Wisdom from heaven leaves doors open: in relationships, in hearts, in
situations. Earthly wisdom closes doors, sometimes forever. We're left
with a sinking feeling of "What if?" If you're like me, you can think of
several times you acted without wisdom and regret it now. Can you
think of the times you acted *with* wisdom? Those stories are sometimes
harder to recollect because they don't leave us with baggage. Heartaches
stay on our minds and wound us for years. Regrets are hard to let go of.
But wisdom brings peace, and even when the outcomes are less than
perfect, we have no regrets. We move on. I've spent many nights agonizing over my poor choices, but when was the last time you couldn't sleep
because you just kept thinking about all your wise choices?

Wisdom gives lasting freedom from regret, although waiting for
wisdom can be painful.

The Price of Wisdom
Every decision costs us something. There is a price for wisdom. The
price for wisdom is often:

- Waiting
- Patience
- Loss of ego and pride
- Humility

God says wisdom will be worth any price, because no amount of material goods can replace her:

> Wisdom is better than all the trappings of wealth;
> nothing you could wish for holds a candle to her.
>
> (PROVERBS 8:11)

The major difference between the cost of wisdom and the cost of foolishness is that wisdom demands we pay now by developing character, and foolishness demands we pay later in consequences. Consequences sting us endlessly, but character brings eternal rewards. This is the life God has prepared for us to lead:

> Everything that goes into a life of pleasing God has been
> miraculously given to us by getting to know, personally
> and intimately, the One who invited us to God.
> The best invitation we ever received! We were
> also given absolutely terrific promises
> to pass on to you—your tickets to participation
> in the life of God after you turned your back on
> a world corrupted by lust.
>
> So don't lose a minute in building on what you've
> been given, complementing your basic faith with good
> character, spiritual understanding, alert discipline,
> passionate patience, reverent wonder, warm
> friendliness, and generous love, each dimension
> fitting into and developing the others.
>
> (2 PETER 1:3-7)

Esther's Legacy of Wisdom

Esther was willing to pay the price for wisdom. She prayed, fasted, and waited three days before her first banquet, and then waited one additional night before making her petition. As a result, she saved a nation. A national holiday was declared to honor her bravery and the salvation of her people. The end of her story was peace, restoration, and joy: peace for her people, reunion with Mordecai, honor from the king, and a big party every year to remember it all.

Two thousand, six hundred years later, we're still celebrating. What a legacy! We don't celebrate her beauty (we don't know what she looked like). We don't celebrate her wealth (we don't know whether Mordecai ever had money). We don't celebrate her romance (we don't even know if she liked the king!). We celebrate her wisdom, which was truly from heaven. Wisdom from heaven is eternal. It never dies, although we do. That's why stories of wisdom survive from generation to generation.

How can you develop a passion for wisdom in yourself—and your daughter? It begins with the spark of stories, stories from Scripture like the book of Esther. It extends to lessons from history, biographies of modern heroines, and stories from your own family. Never stop telling stories.

PREPARING FOR YOUR MEETING

This Month's Beauty Treat: family heirloom jewelry

Wisdom is more precious than jewels, and now is a fine evening to share a precious jewel with your daughter, just as you have now shared with her almost an entire year of family wisdom and stories. Whether it's a little necklace given to you on a long-ago anniversary, or a ring handed down from your own mother, this is the night to share it.

At:

Appointment date and time:

Where we'll eat:

Story Stirrers

1. What was the wisest decision you ever made? How did you make the decision? What was the outcome?

2. When, and why, are you prone to unwise decisions?

3. How do you know what the wise choice is? Do you always know? If you have doubts, what do you do?

4. When have you seen your daughter acting with great wisdom?

Go Back for Seconds

1. Buy a journal to record the stories of faith from your own life and your extended family. Keep this as a legacy for your daughter.

2. Buy her a journal and encourage her to record her own stories.

3. Write to older family members and ask them to contribute one story from their own lives about the power—and price—of wisdom.

PREPARE YOUR DAUGHTER FOR THE ESTHER MEETING

1. We'll be getting together for our Esther Year time on this date and time:
2. This month's beauty treat will be: family heirloom jewelry.
3. This month's story verses are: Esther 5:3-4.
4. So when we're together, we're going to be talking about: wisdom.

Celebrating the Journey's End . . . and Beginning

The Esther Year is the beginning of a lifelong covenant between you and your daughter.

KEY VERSE:
These days are to be remembered and kept by every single generation,
every last family, every province and city. (Esther 9:28)

Esther's story has ended, and your daughter's has just begun. Mom, as you prepare for the final evening with your daughter, I'll help you create a special time for her to join with you to pray for her continued, blessed journey into womanhood. Let's take this last month and celebrate the journey toward becoming a woman. This passage into adulthood is rarely celebrated in the Christian culture. We celebrate grades, games, holidays, and choices, but we don't always celebrate the profound meaning of time's passing. I hope *Queen Esther's Secrets* has been a time of laughter, bonding, a few tears perhaps, and some quiet reflection for you both. Mostly, I hope it has been a source of comfort and blessing for your daughter, a deeply reassuring message that becoming a woman is indeed a wonderful thing.

This year marks a metamorphosis in your daughter's life, and it is no less one for you as well. We've been wrapped up in raising our daughters for so long. Thinking of them as adults who will make their way into the world can be overwhelming. We need to celebrate what we've shared together and remind each other of all the unknown blessings ahead waiting to be discovered. Tonight is the night to celebrate this new passage, the coming metamorphosis that you will both undergo, and the new stories that are about to begin.

I'd like to suggest one thing you can do to commemorate this final evening together. Before every journey, a woman packs, right? Whether it's a suitcase, carry-on, or purse, women understand the need to hold something close as we venture into the unknown. We're packers by nature. We begin motherhood by packing. We pack a hospital bag and keep it by the door. Later we pack a diaper bag and keep it by our side. As our kids get older, we pack lunches, backpacks, and suitcases for summer camp. All of motherhood has prepared us for this: packing the essentials we know she'll need for the adventures ahead.

What is it she will need for the days ahead? What is it you wish that you had been sent out with? This "packing" for the future can take many forms:

- Buy a journal and fill the first few pages with verses of Scripture and inspirational quotes that she'll need. You can separate these out by category: encouragements, affirmations, and faith-builders. Think about the gifts God has given her and the struggles she might still be facing.
- Buy or create a "prayer box" and fill it with pieces of paper naming your wishes and hopes for her future—and leave plenty of room for her to add her own.
- Begin a new tradition tonight that will extend far beyond *Queen Esther's Secrets.* When I grew older, my grandmother began the tradition of giving me a new devotional/inspirational book once every year. She buys one for herself, too, and reads it throughout the year with me. It's her way of helping me "pack" for the year ahead.

The Power of Remembering

God wants us to remember the meaningful moments of our lives, to celebrate and relive our blessings. God especially wants us to remember Him and His role in those blessings:

> Remember the world of wonders he has made,
> his miracles, and the verdicts he's rendered.
>
> (PSALM 105:5)

God remembers us, too:

> The LORD remembers us and will bless us.
>
> (PSALM 115:12, NIV)

Ultimately, the power of memory is for the building up of our faith:

> Remember your history,
> your long and rich history.
> I am GOD, the only God you've had or ever will have—
> incomparable, irreplaceable—
> From the very beginning
> telling you what the ending will be,
> All along letting you in
> on what is going to happen,
> Assuring you, "I'm in this for the long haul,
> I'll do exactly what I set out to do."
>
> (ISAIAH 46:9-10)

Amen! God has known your story long before you came into this world, and He's written a very good ending for it, too. There is no one and no thing like Him. He's with us on this journey, for every step and each mile. We can take hold of our daughter's hand and face tomorrow together, knowing a powerful God overshadows us both with love. May God continue to bless your journey, and thank you for spending a year of it with me! I look forward to hearing about your time with your daughter and will be praying for a rich legacy of memories for you both.

PREPARING FOR YOUR MEETING

This Month's Beauty Treat: a beautiful robe

In biblical times, giving someone a robe was a sign of blessing and of a covenant between you. God gave us a robe when we first trusted Him: "He has wrapped me with a robe of righteousness" (Isaiah 61:10, NASB). Let the robe you give her be a sign of the covenant between you both, a commitment to walk the paths ahead with excellence, honor, and unconditional love.

At:

Appointment date and time:

Where we'll eat:

Story Stirrers

1. Mom, what's on your heart tonight? What has this year meant to you?

2. What changes have you seen in your daughter during her Esther Year?

3. What hopes and dreams do you have for the path ahead in your own adventure? What do you hope is ahead for your daughter?

Go Back for Seconds

1. Create a lasting legacy between you, such as the one my grandmother and I share. What ritual can you create to remind each other of the lessons of the Esther Year?

2. Is there a younger girl at church or school who desperately needs a mentor? Your daughter is ready to share her wisdom and encouragement with the next girl.

PREPARE YOUR DAUGHTER FOR THE ESTHER MEETING

1. We'll be getting together for our Esther Year time on this date and time:
2. This month's beauty treat will be: a beautiful robe.
3. This month's story verse is: Esther 9:28.
4. So when we're together, we're going to be talking about: celebrating the journey's end and a new beginning.

Suggestions for Beauty Treats

If a suggested beauty treat for the month doesn't fit your daughter's age or interest, peek at this list to see if there's a good substitution you can make. Let your daughter's age, preferences, and your budget be your guide. Be sure to budget a few treats for yourself, too!

1. Manicure
2. Pedicure
3. Haircut
4. Highlights or hair color
5. Hair accessories
6. Makeup lesson
7. Skin-care lesson
8. Skin-care product
9. Facial
10. Body lotions and powders
11. Spa massage (shoulder and feet massages are popular, less expensive options than a full-body massage and would be great shared with you, mom!)
12. Wardrobe consultant: how to choose the right clothes for each body type
13. Perfume shopping
14. Color analysis: what colors look best in clothes, accessories, or makeup
15. Jewelry

16. Beauty guides: magazines or books that encourage healthy, godly standards
17. Bath treats: bubble baths, bath salts, fizzies, bath oils
18. Contacts (if your daughter wears glasses)
19. Beautiful robe
20. Boar-bristle hairbrush: Were you told to brush your hair one hundred strokes every night before bed? These vintage rituals have staying power! Boar-bristle brushes last for years and give hair a beautiful sheen.
21. Eyebrow wax: nothing brings out the natural beauty of eyes more than a perfectly shaped brow or better shows her how to complement natural beauty without cosmetics.

Resource Guide

Below are some of my favorite authors and resources. If you are interested in exploring a topic we've covered in *Queen Esther's Secrets* in greater detail, any of these books would be a great place to start.

QUEEN ESTHER
Garrett, Ginger. *Chosen: The Lost Diaries of Queen Esther.* Colorado Springs, CO: NavPress, 2005.

FINANCES
Kay, Ellie. *The Debt Diet: An Easy-to-follow Plan to Shed Debt and Trim Spending.* Bloomington, MN: Bethany House, 2005.

BODY IMAGE AND WEIGHT ISSUES
Arterburn, Stephen and Garrett, Ginger. *Lose It for Life for Teens: The Spiritual, Emotional, and Physical Solution.* Franklin, TN: Integrity, 2004.
Mintle, Dr. Linda. *Making Peace with Your Thighs: Get off the Scales and Get on with Your Life.* Franklin, TN: Integrity, 2006.

PUBERTY/HEALTH
Carter, Carrie, MD. *A Woman's Guide to Good Health.* Oakville, CT: Spire Books, 2006.
*Gravelle, Karen and Gravelle, Jennifer. *The Period Book: Everything You Don't Want to Ask (But Need to Know).* New York: Walkerbooks, 1996.
*Northrup, Christiane, MD. *Mother-Daughter Wisdom: Creating a Legacy of Physical and Emotional Health.* New York: Bantam, 2005.

SEXUALITY AND PURITY

Ethridge, Shannon and Arterburn, Stephen. *Every Woman's Battle: Discovering God's Plan for Sexual and Emotional Fulfillment.* Colorado Springs, CO: WaterBrook, 2003.

Ethridge, Shannon and Arterburn, Stephen. *Every Young Woman's Battle: Guarding Your Mind, Heart, and Body in a Sex-Saturated World.* Colorado Springs, CO: WaterBrook, 2004.

Ethridge, Shannon and Arterburn, Stephen. *Preparing Your Daughter for Every Woman's Battle: Creative Conversations About Sexual and Emotional Integrity.* Colorado Springs, CO: WaterBrook, 2005.

FOR MOMS ONLY

Glickman, Craig. *Solomon's Song of Love: Let the Song of Songs Inspire Your Own Romantic Story.* West Monroe, LA: Howard Publishing, 2003.

PURPOSE

Brazelton, Katie. *Pathway to Purpose for Women: Connecting Your To-Do List, Your Passions, and God's Purposes for Your Life.* Grand Rapids, MI: Zondervan, 2005.

DISCIPLINE

Foster, Richard. *Celebration of Discipline.* San Francisco: HarperSanFrancisco, 1998.

EMOTIONS

Dillow, Linda. *Calm My Anxious Heart: A Woman's Guide to Contentment.* Colorado Springs, CO: NavPress, 1998.

FASTING

Moe, Cynthia. *Hunger Pains: A Woman's Guide to a Spiritual Fast.* Colorado Springs, CO: NavPress, 2006.

FEAR AND FAITH

Crenshaw, Kitty and Snapp, Catherine. *The Hidden Life: Revelations from a Holy Journey.* Colorado Springs, CO: NavPress, 2005.

Kent, Carol. *Tame Your Fears: And Transform Them into Faith, Confidence, and Action.* Colorado Springs, CO: NavPress, 2003.

Kent, Carol. *When I Lay My Isaac Down: Unshakable Faith in Unthinkable Circumstances.* Colorado Springs, CO: NavPress, 2005.

PARENTING

Courtney, Vicki. *Your Girl: Raising a Godly Daughter in an Ungodly World.* Nashville, TN: Broadman & Holman, 2004.

DeMuth, Mary. *Building the Christian Family You Never Had: A Practical Guide for Pioneer Parents.* Colorado Springs, CO: WaterBrook, 2006.

Eller, T. Suzanne. *Real Issues, Real Teens: What Every Parent Needs to Know.* Colorado Springs, CO: LifeJourney, 2002.

Eller, T. Suzanne. *The Mom I Want to Be: Rising Above Your Past to Give Your Children a Greater Future.* Eugene, OR: Harvest House, 2006.

Elmore, Tim. *Nurturing the Leader Within Your Child: What Every Parent Needs To Know.* Nashville, TN: Nelson, 2001.

FOR TEENS ONLY

Courtney, Vicki. *Teenvirtue: Real Issues, Real Life . . . A Teen Girl's Survival Guide.* Nashville, TN: Broadman & Holman, 2005.

* These books are not written from an explicitly Christian point of view, but they do contain a wealth of valuable information.

Acknowledgments

This book would not have been possible without the following people:

My husband, who lives with the abundance of estrogen in his household with humor and grace. Growing up, my brother warned me I'd have a hard time finding a man because a lot of men don't like strong women. Thankfully, he was right. Mitch was everything worth waiting for.

My agent, Lee Hough, who is trustworthy and wise. He is an excellent literary shepherd for this sheep so easily bedazzled by new pastures.

My publishers at NavPress, including Darla Hightower, Melanie Knox, Terry Behimer, Dan Rich, Kent Wilson, Kris Wallen, Jessica Chappell, Kate Berry, Nicci Hubert, the incredible sales team: Eric Helus, Pamela Mendoza, Christine Corbett, Sheila Dean, Becky Martinez, Erin Shank, Valerie Werckle, Toby Lorenc, Heather Hebert, Brent Klassen, Michele McGuire, Candis Pflueger, and Sean Mitchell. Publishing with you has been one of the greatest experiences of my career. My writing career and my spirit have benefited from knowing you more than I can express.

And especially Andrea Christian, who has been my agent, publicist, editor, and always my friend. You're younger than me (drats!) but so wise, and so deeply infused with the spirit of Christ, that I find myself admiring you more every year.

And my Esther Year team: Donna Ham, Susan Lang, Rita Bailey, Carolynn James, Grandmother Eloise, and my own mom Carole

Garrett, plus the many women who contributed to the project by filling out surveys for me.

First Christian Church: Penny, Robin, Peggy, Betsy, Tammy. I owe each of you a debt of gratitude for your support, teaching, and a quiet place to write where I am free from the lures of e-mail, phones, and the fridge.

Notes

How to Lead Your Daughter Through Queen Esther's Secrets

1. Jane Weaver, "What Are Our Dating Pet Peeves?" May 2005, accessed on April 19, 2006 at http://www.msnbc.msn.com/id/7736649/.

Month Two

1. Anne Trippe, *Marriage! The Journey* (Ontario: Essence Publishing, 2004), 33.
2. Trippe, 39.
3. "Family Day: A Day to Eat Dinner With Your Children," accessed on April 19, 2006 at http://www.girlpower.gov/AdultsWhoCare/general/familyday.htm.

Month Three

1. Christiane Northrup, MD, Excerpt from *Mother-Daughter Wisdom*, chapter 1, pages 3–4, retrieved at http://www.drnorthrup.com/womens-health-mdwisdom.php.
2. "Meditation Changes Brains," *ScienCentral News*: 8/5/03, available at www.sciencentral.com/articles.
3. Carol Krucoff, "Exercise & PMS," iVillage Health, accessed on April 19, 2006 at http://health.ivillage.com/gyno/gynoperiod/0,4mc3,00.ht.
4. "The Human Brain/Renew-Sleep and Stress," The Franklin Institute Online, accessed on April 19, 2006 at http://fi.edu/brain/sleep.htm.

Month Five

1. Jackie Hatton, "Flappers," *The St. James Encyclopedia of Pop Culture*, 2002, Gale Group.
2. Joan Jacobs Brumberg, *The Body Project: An Intimate History of American Girls* (New York: Random House, First Vintage Books Edition, 1998), 4.

Month Seven

1. Curt Suplee, "Stressed Women Turn to Mother Nurture," *Washington Post*, May 19, 2000. accessed on March 16, 2006 at http://www.montgomerycollege.edu/faculty/~dfox/public_html/stressedwomen.htm.
2. Craig Glickman, *Solomon's Song of Love* (West Monroe, LA: Howard Publishers, 2003), 144.
3. Robert E. Rector, Kirk A. Johnson, PhD, and Lauren R. Noyes, "Sexually Active Teenagers Are More Likely to Be Depressed and to Attempt Suicide," Center for Data Analysis Report #03-04, accessed on April 19, 2006 at www.heritage.org/research/Family/cola0304.cfm.
4. Angie Vineyard, "Protection Teens Are Still Not Getting" Dec. 19, 2002, accessed on May 2, 2005 at http://www.beverlylahayeinstitute.org/articledisplay.asp?id=2944&department=BLI&categoryid=femfacts.
5. The National Campaign to Prevent Teen Pregnancy, accessed on April 19, 2006 at www.Teenpregnancy.org/resources/reading/pdf/35percent.pdf.

Month Eight

1. Harriet Lerner, PhD, *The Dance of Fear* (New York: Perennial Currents, 2005), 173.
2. Gavin de Becker, *Protecting the Gift* (New York: The Dial Press/ Random House, 1999), 201.

Month Nine

1. Rick Warren, *The Purpose-Driven Life* (Grand Rapids, MI: Zondervan, 2002), 17-18.
2. "Teen Girls Get Pregnant Intentionally Without Other Attainable Life Goals," *Cornell Science News*: June 4, 1997. Accessed on February 27, 2006 at www.news.cornell.edu/releases/June97/ teenpregnancy.ssl.html.

Author

GINGER GARRETT is the author of the acclaimed novel *Chosen: The Lost Diaries of Queen Esther* and the *Serpent Moon Trilogy*. Her hobbies include exploring the lives of ancient women and making relevant connections to today's culture. She also loves chocolate, giant dogs, and giggling girls. She is the mom of two daughters and one son. You can visit her website at www.gingergarrett.com.

Watch for **GINGER GARRETT'S**
newest release from Nelson Books

IN STORES SEPTEMBER 2007

Beauty Secrets of the Bible
THE ANCIENT ARTS OF BEAUTY AND FRAGRANCE

In her forthcoming book, Ginger reveals how
every woman can accent her God-given beauty, using
the hidden treasures of the ancient scriptures—where
every scent and every act of beautification had
spiritual and emotional significance.

Ginger's new book will not only give you the *Biblical
history* of beauty but also the way to natural health
and economical alternatives to high-priced
department store beauty products.

You will lean how to create your own beauty
regimen based on the ancient products
and techniques Ginger uncovers in the Bible.

Embrace your unique physical beauty!

IT IS GOD'S GIFT TO YOU!

ISBN: 0-7852-2178-6
$13.99 TRADE PAPER

INTRODUCING THE SERPENT MOON TRILOGY, BY GINGER GARRETT.

Dark Hour

1-57683-869-2

Join Ginger Garrett in *Dark Hour*, the first episode in the SERPENT MOON trilogy as she tells an expertly woven tale of stunning betrayal, bloodthirsty revenge, and a fiery passion, all setting the stage for an epic story of mothers and daughters, sisters and brothers, husbands and wives.

Midnight Throne

1-57683-870-6

Available September 2007

King Ahab lost his heart to the wrong woman—and sacrificed his kingdom. Torn between living for God and loving his forbidden bride, Ahab battled the darkness at war with his conscience. Only one man had the power to save him from his bride, but would Elijah condemn him for his weakness?

Huntress Night

1-57683-871-4

Available May 2008

A cautionary tale of the war between our call to greatness and our darkest secrets. The story of Delilah's betrayal is still whispered today, but did you know there were three women involved in the serpent's plot to seduce and destroy the greatest of the Judges? Sampson would love one, marry another, and destroy them all.

Visit your local Christian bookstore,
call NavPress at 1-800-366-7788, or log on to www.navpress.com.
To locate a Christian bookstore near you, call 1-800-991-7747.